MOVING TO NEPTUNE

New & Selected

EARL S. BRAGGS

ANHINGA PRESS
TALLAHASSEE, FLORIDA 2023

Cover photograph: "Moving" by Earl S. Braggs

Cover design: Carol Lynne Knight

Author photo: Natalie Braggs

Text design and production: Carol Lynne Knight

Type Styles: Titles are set in Neue Kabel;
text is set in Adobe Garamond Premiere

Library of Congress Cataloging-in-Publication Data

"Moving to Neptune: New and Selected," by Earl S. Braggs, First Edition

ISBN – 978-1-934695-67-8

Library of Congress Cataloging Card Number – 2023939144

Anhinga Press Inc. is dedicated wholly to the
publication and appreciation of fine poetry and other literary genres.

For personal orders, catalogs and information write to:
Anhinga Press
P.O. Box 3665
Tallahassee, Florida 32315
Website: www.anhingapress.org
Email: info@anhinga.org

Published in the United States
by Anhinga Press
Tallahassee, Florida
First Edition, 2023

PRAISE FOR THE POETRY OF EARL S. BRAGGS

At the intersection of black and white, fish and snakes, rural and city, poor and more poor, public and private, *Boy Named Boy* names what it means to live out loud, Black, shamelessly declaring restorative witness ... This memoir of race and survival croons and scrutinizes a sultry but sharp Southern manner.

— *Jaki Shelton Green, Poet Laureate of North Carolina (2018-2020)*

Like notes of jazz ... *Obama's Children* is a headlong riff on the motifs of race, history, legacy and love ... a sparkling magnum opus.

— *Gianna Russo*

In *Negro Side of the Moon,* Earl S. Braggs confronts the problem of the color line with lyrical ferocity and politically charged wit. ... *Negro Side of the Moon* is an invitation to all of us to wake the hell up and take a long [take those sunglasses off] look at what ails the American psyche.

— *Tim Seibles, Poet Laureate of Virginia (2018-2020)*

What is and has always been needed is an honest, clear, loving voice. Earl Braggs' *Ugly Love (Notes from the Negro Side of the Moon)* offers that. Pull up your favorite chair and cover your cold feet with your grandmother's quilt and enjoy this wonderful read.

— *Nikki Giovanni*

... these large, vivid, Kerouacian, music saturated poems. The reader is returned, through repetition's felicities — the epic extension of the moment of composition — inward to our national soul.

— *Alice Notley*

Earl S. Braggs' *Crossing Tecumseh Street* is lively, vocal, and laced with an intelligent sense of humor. I enjoyed these poems.

— *Billy Collins, Poet Laureate of the United States (2001-2003)*

Powered by an incantatory rhythm in the tradition of Whitman..., Braggs takes us across *Crossing Tecumseh Street* into a world of dazzling visions, enormous disappointment and guarded hope.

— *Richard Jackson*

Walking Back from Woodstock — No romanticism here, but a witnessing with wit and irony, with subtle wisdom that rises only out of the fire.

— *Christopher Buckley*

In *Hats,* Braggs powerfully bears testimony of the country's disenfranchised in rolling headlong cadences that aspire to the incantatory. They also register leaping exuberance, joy, spiritual yearning, and the majesty of enduring.

— *Lynda Hull*

Cruising Weather Wind Blue confronts us with a combination of hard realism and musical lyricism. ...This is American poetry at its finest: as spacious as Walt Whitman, as frank as the Beat poets ... Braggs is a master storyteller.

— *source unknown*

OTHER BOOKS BY EARL S. BRAGGS

Boy Named Boy (a Memoir)
Wet Cement Press

Obama's Children
Madville Publishing

Cruising Weather Wind Blue
Anhinga Press

Hat Dancing Blue with Miss Bessie Smith
Yellow Jacket Press

Negro Side of the Moon
C&R Press

Ugly Love
C&R Press

Oliver's Breakfast in America
Eureka Press

Syntactical Arrangement of a Twisted Wind
Anhinga Press

Younger Than Neil
Anhinga Press

In Which Language Do I keep Silent
Anhinga Press

Crossing Tecumseh Street
Anhinga Press

House on Fontanka
Anhinga Press

Walking Back from Woodstock
Anhinga Press

Hat Dancer Blue
Anhinga Press

Hats
Linprint Press

This book is dedicated

to

Natalie, Rashida, and Anastasiya Braggs

THE PUBLICATION OF THIS BOOK IS SUPPORTED

BY A GENEROUS DONATION FROM

LAVINIA JOHNSTON

CONTENTS

ACKNOWLEDGMENTS

"Obama's Children," reprinted, with permission, from *Obama's Children* (Madville Publishing, 2021).

"The Weight of Not Answering," appeared in the anthology, *RUMORS SECRETS & LIES* (Anhinga Press, 2022)

Autumn Avenue: "The Half Life of Chocolate

Vox Populi: "Such is the Love Story of Sally"

WCP Magazine: "Late for School Again Today"

LIKE A FISHING LINE THROUGH LILYPADS: THE POETRY OF EARL S. BRAGGS

Neptune is the Roman god of waters and seas, and as such he controlled the winds and storms. So does Earl Braggs, in events, history, education and, overtly and inherently, music:

- If poetry is music, Earl Braggs is its composer. And what he composes is jazz — smoky, sensual, serpentine stanzas of jazzy poetry at its improvisational best ...

For his most recent volume, *Obama's Children*, the above is an excerpt from a blurb I provided. After having read the poems in *Moving to Neptune*, I see nothing that would prompt me to alter the truth of that assertion. To the contrary, jazz, along with an occasional suffusion of the blues, not only crops up repeatedly as subject matter but defines both the structure and the syntax and language of the poems and the book as a whole. Mainly, the poems are narrative, but lyrically-driven and diverse in diction, rhythm, melody and harmony, just like jazz "touching me and all of us like Thelonious / Monk touching a piano baseball, hitting homeruns / on a trumpet like Dizzy Gillespie. ..."

That Braggs is his own jazz master is evident from the get-go. Unlike the usual Selected Poems arrangements — most recent to most distant; most distant to most recent — for *Moving to Neptune,* he arranges to accommodate the through lines of the poems themselves, how they follow and play off each other. Poems from any given volume of his fifteen collections to date appear at one point, then later, at another. In other words, structurally

2

planned thematically, Braggs is improvising, just like in jazz. Call it the literary version of melodic repetition, something jazz incorporates, with endlessly playful riffing variations, of course; or again, as I put it in my blurb, "staccato-trumpeting lines, tempo-driven voices, melodic repetitions, lowdown bluesy fragmentations of logic and sensibility. ..."

Improvisation is a kind of play, and so is the poetic use of language. To a poet like Braggs language is everything, its sound and its sense, and his is a linguistic medium of propulsion, the play of words super-heated, again in both sound and sense, much like jazz. In a poem that lauds his teachers, though he has them collectively admonishing him for his errors in an essay, those very errors are in fact some of the tools he uses to, as the great Gwendolyn Brooks says, push the language, make it out-perform itself.:

But Earl you
use too many commas,
 too many spliced-up splices,
 too many misplaced conjunctions coordinating
 too many loose ends, untied without purpose,
too descriptive, your description in
too many places,
too many construction splits, confusing shifts,
too many dangling modifiers
and misplaced modifiers modifying
misplaced words like some misplaced somebody

3

looking for something
misplaced like misplaced love.

Too many? *Au contraire, mes professeurs.* Not only does Braggs dare to use any of these he deems necessary to his poems, he piles up words like a hundred-car crash on the Interstate. That's the kind of poet he is — like one of the early jazz maestros, a risk-taker in his language use, but always driven by a sense of play and purpose, stretching out the sound and sense like a jazz man, a note to the breaking point, always urging it to out-perform itself.

Jazz runs through *Moving to Neptune* like a fishing line through lily pads — you can't always see it, but it's there, dangling its smoky lure, enticing a reader's ears. You can feel it, sense it, your whole body vibrant and attuned to its riffs and runs. In the title poem, an open invitation to the reader to kick back and swing to the hot as pepper sprouts band, to revel in the sultry sounds of Rollins, Mingus, Roach, Monk — and Lester Young, who we are told is "moving to Neptune."

Come on in, the speaker says, come on in and join the party. We don't even have to knock: John Coltrane will answer the door," and who knows, Billie or Etta or Ella or Nina might be there, Billie passing out her signature white carnation. So go on, take the sensuous bait, tongue that smoky lure and let the music reel you in. It's clear, in this scat-singing collection of selected poems Earl Braggs is both the host and the jazz band grooving to a sound all its own.

And what a band it is!

— George Drew

MOVING TO NEPTUNE

NEW & SELECTED

MOVING TO NEPTUNE

Those who were seen dancing were thought to be insane
by those who could not hear the music.
— Nietzche

for the room of jazz, where Richard Paul Lives

And before you knock, Blue Train, John Coltrane will
answer the door. And before you enter, Etta James or
Ella Fitzgerald or Nina Simone, one of which will whisper
ever so softly, "I've been expecting you." So come in into

the *relax* of a good red wine year. Pour for yourself, a glass.
Gouda and good green olives will pour, for you, the next
set designed not in Hollywood but, still
triangled in mid-century style conversations with Art Deco
and Marilyn Monroe, a vintage couch, a chair,
a coffee table, a white fireplace, burning
in the soft-wind-falling float of melodies soaring like kites
ascending ceiling height,
just above the cruising altitude of love and forgiveness.

Me and my Uncle Lee, who invited us in? We are having
another sip of red, tasting the room temperature of things
yet to be heard. Listen, but with your ears, listen not,
for only the heart's wall can hear the jazz soaring
into the slow moon dance of "Where the Wind Comes From"

that blows, kindly, "The Sailboat in the Maple Tree"

so dizzy ing ly, intriguingly beautiful, by now, you have been
hyp-no-tized into forgetting why, into this room,   you came.

But we ain't forgot nothing yet.   "'Round About Midnight,",
me and my Uncle Willie Lee, drunk as two pints of moonshine
disguised as sunshine gin,   the geography of a quart of jazz.

The street level MARQUEE, no need to be.   Nothing but
neon lights and constellations full of blue   Negro stars
in a Colored people's night sky:

On vocals,   Miss Billie Holiday, white carnation in her hair,
her red dress,   dancing like wind, ironing it's own
wrinkles out and about, into a cigarette smokey   breeze.

On tenor sax, Sonny Rollins, rolling-solo his way out into
outer space,   racing against phases of a storm-shy moon
soon   as not soon at all   in a room like this.

On drums, Maxwell Roach, beating holes into the toes of
a brand-new pair of miss-matched, checkerboard socks lost
in the washing machine,   but not lost at all
in the rent-to-own   -never-will-be-paid-for-on-time dryer.

On upright bass, Charlie Mingus, ten Negro fingers showing
four steel strings how to   make paper money change church
Sunday-morning collection paper plate paper denominations.

On piano, Thelonious Monk, pine top hat slanted on his head,
knocking out, cold   black and   white keys like he's wearing
boxing gloves outside of a boxing ring. "*It don't mean a thing
if it ain't got that swing.*"

And on tenor sax on a regular night,   but on clarinet tonight,
Prez, the President, some say the night's favorite,   Lester Young,

in the backroom,   looking for a pawn shop ticket stub
in the cool brown eyes of   "Stella by Starlight,"
packing all his shit   in one beat-up,   tied together suitcase.

If the Greyhound bus can get him   at least   part-way there
and he don't need no   Negro-visa   stamped   passport,
tomorrow morning early, before
the rooster crows,   Lester Young is moving to Neptune.

TONIGHT, I DO NOT WANT TO WRITE ANYMORE

The mathematics of love is always uneven.
Why then so tragically
beautifully in this room, your voice
reading to me on remembered nights of white satin,
a Russian love story, The Master and his Margarita?

I did not listen, I did not know how to listen
to the way Rachmaninoff drenched sheets
of piano music down upon us all night long until
Sergei's Russian rainstorm stopped playing our song.

I guess, at some point, we all wait until it's almost
too late to learn how to spell LOVE.

"What We Talk About When We Talk About Love,"
that Raymond Carver short story that fits now
so perfectly now

into the size of your high heel shoes, so neatly
placed, now, in high heel shoeboxes stacked,
on top of suitcases and other untried cases of
togetherness disguised as unforgiveness.

Moving-out boxes and carelessly packed tote bags
waiting at the front door now trying
to get out of the front door without allowing
my tears to see they, too, are now crying rivers
between leaving me and loving you. Windpipe

music whispering inaudible nothingness into
the somethingness of nothing left to be said.

My mother never told me not to play in wet streets,
so now I walk the architectural designs of Falling
Water. I love, we both love Frank Lloyd Wright
and the slant of his love, his cool October hat. But
September that year remembers, now, nothing
about the nights when it did not rain. Greta Garbo
would know, but
we forgot we never did quite finish watching
her last silent picture show.

Black and white love top shelf drunk,
still drinking. Clinking, me and you, two blue glasses,
cerulean blue, a corner cafe table made for two.
I remember your eyes, your face and how they spoke
so amazingly wonderful without saying a word.

The audience had to guess. And yes,
I did not listen. I did not know how
to listen to the way Orion pulls Neptune so close
to her breast on so many rainy Russian nights.

You love the moon and the moon loves you even on
wet-street nights when wet streets
reflect the reverse of what it sees in puddles of
understanding how honestly twisted
love can sometimes feel on turquoise twisted evenings.
Somebody said, Van Gogh said, "Yellow is the color of
love." How can I disagree, how can anyone disagree

with the holes in the knees of your Levi's
still thrown across our bedroom chair, staring at me.

I now see how and what and why streetlights
don't really love anybody and why stars change
constellations when we are not looking. I wonder
if the books you left on our blue bookshelf miss
the way you always intended to read each of them.

Remember our evenings when we drank
Handel's Water Music,
Remember us chasing the sky,
flying kites, walking in rain in the afternoon,
jumping puddle of left-over morning moments of
love and magic. But now
by the time we look back it has already disappeared.

Tonight, here in what once was our yellow room, every
now or then a yellow cab laughs at the lateness of
the night. A freight train in the distance wails lonesome
the end of a story without a beginning. Because

I prefer the tantalizing perfume of fresh cut flowers,
tonight I do not want to write anymore. I want
to sleep in the Queen's bed with you, my love, my dear

Odessa morning breeze.

I wanta love you like science, like geography.
Like a cartographer in love with the color of yellow

pencils, I want to map-make a picture of you
in a foreign language in a foreign country
on a foreign afternoon
on the edge of Spain in the South of France.

I wanta dance with you like a Russian romance novel,
Lara and Yuri,
Doctor Zhivago. I know, but I cannot bring
myself to read. I need a drink.
I do not want to think about anything but you,

you promenading along Nevsky Prospect Street.

You, dancing the balance of Akhmatova's pure wind.
You, measuring the gaze of a skyline full of stars.
You, holding hands with the moon and Joseph Brodsky
and me.
You, wearing a winter-white St. Peterburg winter coat.
You, wearing the night around your shoulders like it
was made for you.

NO ONE ASKED ABOUT THE WAY I WAS DRESSED

Long before we hear it, another bomb will fall.
knowing this I keep still
here among the rumors.
I have fallen in love with winter.

If we were lovers in this war torn city
would the clocks tell the low dishonest truth
to each of us
sleeping the seats of this low dishonest bus?
Would they tell to each of us the narrowness of
our yesterdays?

From a window in the rear of a yellow dishonest room,
I look for patterns of flights in mid-flight. It's midnight
and I've come back to this, my immigration city.

Darkness stares from everywhere, sees everything.
In the street, where they fall they stay, everyday, children
and babies. Milk bottles that refuse to spill still
empty white.

It occurs to me now that bombs dig ditches and plant
holes beside churches and around monuments,
that a regiment bivouacs on the Rhine, that snipers sleep
on the very edge of tall buildings.

One war started here in this city. How many nights
will it take?

Vineyards run evenly along ravines. Snow whips
the wind back.
Young boys carry oblique weaponry. Night stops here,
silent, at stoplights. Fragmented, cloudy skies forget
to remember, but
the rain in this city forgets nothing.
The brave ones disappear before they know it.
The ones of us who are left disappear, but we know it.
You and I sit somewhere
in se-pa-rated rooms shaking   to be together.
Before we know it another bomb will fall.

One by one I have forgotten the last of the soldier girls,
the openness of a military V cut, the unzipped pleasure of
down zipping a brown skirt,
I have forgotten it all.
I carry, now, a picture of you. Olive with hair trying not to be
dark red. Beautiful.

If we were lovers in this war-torn city, would we choose
to love in my unsafe room or would we choose to love
at all?
Would our kisses, close misses, be afraid of interruption,
interrogation, the integration of parts inside of
a movie projector that makes black
and white movies so much better when there is no color
to speak not of   like love?

Who then, among us, possesses this camera, this black
and white film?
Who then, among us, frames us in this black

and white war? Who develops
such immigration photographs in milk factories
and process labs?   The question of clothes is upon us.

I wear my jacket everyday blue with a velvet collar.
My pants, ordinary
pale yellow winter plaid, my boots brown and unpolished.
My nationality
is often subject to suspicion and my passport passes only
on occasion
it has been much easier to calculate the rate of my fate.

No one asked about the way I was dressed, so I signed my name
as another. I never asked to be the enemy. I never asked
that my courtyard be shaded
by grapevines of immigration. I asked, only, not to be identified.

If we were lovers in this war-torn city, would the faces of
burnt-out candles give to us slow permission?
Would the long sounds of air raids suddenly steal permission away?
What would your father say? What would he do, what
would your mother think?

If we were lovers in this war-torn city, would we lock the doors
of unsafe rooms?
Would we remember the fields now beneath snow?
Would the snow-covered naked darkness reveal
or would the soft sweet sounds swallow the echoes of bombs

and trucks and tanks and children who still play
in streets where they fall,   they stay?

Platoons form and march. Planes touch and go. Helicopters
hover over
unspilled, spoiled milk. Daylight comes, but night does not
move over.
Nothing good is soon. The moon has been never afraid of the dark.

If we were lovers in this war-torn city, would unsafe rooms tell
the unsafe secret?
Would dead dark cloud-colored bombs rain?
Would a winter overcast sky full of parachutes snow?
Would our slow dance come stray as a stray bullet
we both saw coming   but decided not to move?

STEVE'S SHORT SLEEVE SHIRT

Steve's short sleeve shirts were almost always cut-off,
winter plaid,
flannel shirts as if he knew a next winter
might not come.
Back in '71, he grew an ugly afro that
he couldn't figure out how to be proud of, too thin to hold
an afro pick. We were riot-night running buddies,
best friends in the best of times, the worst of times.

We rode the same dull pencil yellow school bus
during those turbulent school-house years. Our English teacher,
Mrs. Davis, we loved
like young boys love pretty teachers, but
Mrs. Davis wasn't pretty. White as composition notebook
pages, she taught the deconstruction of complex sentences
written in black and white and red.

Unfazed by head rags of race war, she stole our attention,
kept it, never intending to give attention back. We didn't
want it back, anyway. She loved Steve, I loved Steve. We all did.

Steve didn't grow up with us. He moved from the country
to the city our freshman year. Project still-life, still, somewhat,
new. The comprehension of such, I don't think he ever, fully,
wanted to figure out how to measure. Steve was beyond.

Steve was the most honest person I ever knew. One day
during the quiet-riot time of a yesterday or the day

before a yesterday,
Steve and I roamed, randomly, downtown as we so often
did, in and out of stores and shops that had no need
to see us, serve us, give us the time of a weekday. That day

I decided to steal a pocket knife. It was not glued down.
Steve's voice frowned ever so godly upon me, "Put it back."
Putting it back quickly, slowly
I said, "No one's looking, no one saw me." "I saw you,"
Steve said, "I saw you."

That was to be the last time any of us war-street danced
slow with Steve. The Wilmington Star News knew then
of the killing we could not bring ourselves to believe.

He wasn't on the school bus that Thursday morning
after the Wednesday night fire. Fire truck sirens
were everywhere every night. Ordinary,
another ordinary day. I wasn't worried, none of us were.

Many school day mornings, we missed one school bus,
then took another. Mostly, we
were never late for school. Mostly, we
were good students. Mostly we
were good government-housing-projects-life kids

during those riot torn years of city police helicopters feeding
teargas to automobiles
our crying eyes could not afford. Somehow dingy white,
wet towels found a way to disguise us
as young Palestinian war-street boys and the "wetness" saved

us most curfew, moonless nights. But then came
that night that was not so kind to Steve, not to kind to us.

Steve was brilliant, a genius. He knew the answers
to questions before questions were asked, but
he didn't know the mathematics
of his own life,
didn't know how to calculate that   that white policeman
knew how cut-off short
his short-sleeved life was "projected" to be. Somehow

Steve didn't know the bright bullet light-weight of
a house fire
that night would ignite, without white apology, his shirt,
illuminating so un-beautifully in Negro-ghetto colored
tragic hue, a weekday Funeral Announcement with his name on it.

LIKE MAGRITTE, *THIS IS NOT A PIPE*

LIKE ME, *THIS IS NOT A POLITICAL LOVE POEM*

When power narrows the area of man's concerns, poetry reminds him of the richness and diversity of existence.

— John F. Kennedy

for all who were my teachers and still are

Let me ask you this. Does a night sky full of first grade constellations
know how bright they can shine if their first-grade teacher is not looking
at how a magic moons changes tides of small voices? Astronomy love, I

know but since the sky, now, leans on the shoulders of my words, I don't
know if Picasso or even Vincent Van Gogh would've painted what I, now,

see from my window. A plot or not? The Assassination of Education,
seemingly, so proudly penciled-in then printed on leaning, red billboard
freeway signs around the corner from, seemingly, everywhere in America.
No crime, they say, to speak not of. Still, the story to be told below is true.

Somebody is trying to kill the art of teaching. I know who it is, do you
remember your 11th grade English teacher? I do. I remember my love of
the voice of a not-so-pretty, beautiful white woman with a Negro smile
while preaching from the pulpit of William Shakespeare *To be or not to be.*

Miss Irene Davis looked, somewhat stubbornly so, just like an 11th grade
English teacher, cat-eye-librarian black glasses sliding down her pointed,
working class, Birmingham, England, English nose. Her hazel eyes, forever,

singing *Twelfth Night,* Act 1, Scene 1, "If music be the food of love, play on." Sheet music scattered, symphonic in the way she walked adrift a classroom floor. Do you remember the waltz of her words dancing across fifth-period pages of finally understanding *The Catcher in the Rye* and why, so deeply, you fell in love with the slanted angst of Holden Caulfield's red hunting hat?

That memory, yes, but not now from stained stained-glass windows that see us before we hear them parade-marching not to the drum beats of names, but to the drum beats of numbers. All along the way, rumors of reading-trees, now, tremble. Walk with me pace-fully, see if you can hear what a young tree feels when it falls. Love, somebody is trying to kill the art of teaching.

Remember my coach, Mr. Willie E. McGee. Like a medical school professor, he coached the science of singing a strike 3 call. He taught us how to perform surgery on the seams of a baseball. Every day, Coach Willie E. re-measured the baseball-bat-weight of our school paper, paperweight love of the game.

Remember that first day of class when you were the teacher. Remember that lectern, the tilt of, watching you watch desk-rows of young faces watching how dark the room was and stayed until you figured out how to flip on, turn bright the lights, the eyes of young learning-tree smiles. You smiled then, too, didn't you, to the sound waves of young tree-light years.

But, Now, these days, no surprise is also a surprise in classrooms of noise. Cacophony. Listen to the hungry hills of red carpenter ants and flying bees. Listen to the swarming hard-hat-hammers of carpenters un-building HOUSE after HOUSE of EDUCATION. Carpenter ants, carpenter bees drilling into the young years of young wood. Neither of which, desire a *desire* to know the number of bricks needed to construct an elementary school.

Let us now remember what my philosophy professor said when he said, "Go to the window, look out. Just because I say the sky is blue does not make the sky blue." Professor Dr. Denis Robbins. He called himself a boy, a Jewish boy from Brooklyn. And he lectured us just like a Jewish boy from Brooklyn when he said, "Aesthetics is the definition of *you* standing on the bow of a sinking ship rocking back and forth rolling side to side. Biblical waves splashing, crashing, slapping *you* in *your* face facing the drop-dead middle of a black, August night hurricane without an eye to see what *you* cannot hear, your fear wrapped in backdrops of Brahams'

piano keys playing C-sharp minor black coffee black, brewing sheet music disguised as sideways-wind-blowing-rain. The Sea Salt Goddess of Thunder thundering in stereo, dramatizing stage-side edges of a radio sky set design. Debussy electricity, lightning bolts of Pyro-tectonic-symphonic-soundtrack explosions, everywhere." "Aesthetics," he said is *you* at that ship-sinking moment, shaking like theater opening night stage fright, falling, for the first time, in love with the beautifully orchestrated bad beauty of bad weather love."

No, he didn't say it exactly like that, but he did say it exactly like that every Tuesday and Thursday that semester from 9:25 to 10:40 AM when-then that Jewish boy from Brooklyn took me and all of us to "church." Not one of us missed a single class that semester." I can still hear him say, "I'm not here to teach you, I'm here to love you. Love will teach you." Again, no, he didn't say it, but the ghost of what he did say, every day we heard every word. The path to Poursville passes a cornfield, he never did say.

Anyway, today, let us walk on into what, now, has become a beautifully gray afternoon. Let's go catch a movie. Dreary, the weather, another weather-perfect movie set day. It's raining things we cannot name, but the weather channel-weather lady has decided against wearing a raincoat with rainboots. So, let's go get soaking wet in the art of everything left.

The box office window knows our names. Popcorn, lots of butter, Coke in a cup recognize the way we stand in line, waiting to see the marquee:

To Sir, With Love, a British drama film starring Sydney Poitier, 1967. The setting: A rough London East End high school, a rude classroom full of working class, mostly white juvenile delinquents rejected by the walls of an old, worn out, red-brick school building, red-brick shabby, rundown running into the long, quiet arms of a teacher, an American Negro wearing a Windsor-tied necktie with a brown English tweed jacket. Handsome, he is, standing tall behind an oak antique desk, upon which scattered nothing but a satchel, a blue roll-call book, two yellow pencils. And then, floating just above the quiet emptiness of empty space, perfectly un-perfectly placed, not visible to the naked eye, *The Book of Zen* turning school paper pages, one at a time, into the look of twenty-seven love letters, stamped, addressed

To Sir, With Love

—Edward Earl Sherman Braggs II, Composer

LATE FOR SCHOOL AGAIN TODAY

*(A Photograph: An Israeli Settler Protects His Daughter
During an Attack on the Road Linking the Crossing Between ...)*

On a road crossing the desert pastures of Palestine,
a no-stop-street STOP
sign stops

foot traffic in its tracks, turns
with Holy quiet
anticipation,

faces faces, face to face, so close to the impending
to see what impends,
unbuttons

the top button of a suicide vest and blasts into
oblivion
the slow science of walking to school.

No school bus to ride suicide. My father and I,
we walked this morning into
the evil blue breasts of a vest

disguised by the makeup of a made-up
pretty woman without.
Detonation: fresh green butter

beans blasted into split peas,
still green, between
the East Bank and the West Bank of no

river to speak Holy of.
Market day,
ordinary,

market square fully aware without
being fully aware. Ugly
love in the pretty eyes of an ugly,

cloudy,
maybe-it-won't-rain today.
God must be still asleep.

We keep still, my father and I. Leaf
shaking, without a tree, we, stranded beneath
a vegetable stand table. Overly ripe

avocadoes implode, guacamole-cilantro.
Onions, diced, sliced
twice like a salad. Carrots, cabbages blasted

into cabbage slaw. Cucumbers, celery,
olives, white grapes, all bleed red. Dead
red potatoes, dead

chicken feather broth,
tomatoes stewed into
dead homemade soup. Harmonic,

a morning menu of un unlucky breakfast.
We keep still.
I can feel fear in the length of

my father's beard, longer than my hair,
my life.
His wife, my mother, a woman my father loved

beyond mistake. Promises, now, so uneven,
so Holy unreal.
The air smells like dead people's smoke.

My watch
chokes to tick. I am late for school.
I can hear bells ringing in my ear.

Here, life is a step-stop stone
in an ancient city of two Gods, one sun
and one moon.

Soon seems not to know how to forget
or forgive. But
how can any God ask anybody

to settle for this life where children fall,
children stay.
Every day we walk to school between

borders and bombs
and stray bullets
with our names already written in roll books.

I am 15 years old,
I am Jewish,
I am a pretty girl without the makeup

my father does not allow. We're settlers,
we've settled into the sounds
of war auditorium music: Mother, dead.

I was 5. Weathered sandpaper
has rounded off the blasted sharp edges of
this, a table we now perch beneath,

clinging to despair disguised as hope,
watching apples trade
stock market prices with oranges.

100% Juice, a tin can rolling down
the sad but shady
side of the road. A bicycle frame with no

front tire can't see its back wheel
still spinning
slower and slower and slower.

Only the children know all too well,
never,
it will stop turning over

the dead face of no promise of peace
on this earth. Blasted
blind, blinded,

a man pats the sacred ground around
his left foot,
looking for his wedding ring

finger. Smiling iceberg lettuce burned
in place.
God awful smoke music.

Shaking, still, we keep perfectly,
leaning away
from the ills of invented

hate. Late for school, crammed into
the perfect pocket of
a nylon suicide vest. There will be no test

today, no final exit examination,
no answers,
no questions, no nothing but God

forsaken, God awfully bad poetry
blasted into
the blown up, bulletproof margins of
bulletproof paper.

MARLENE DIETRICH (A LOVE STORY)

Trying to remember that movie we watched, but never did finish

German green bedroom eyes is all I recall. But then again maybe
I am just dream-remembering the placid painted color of green

motel room walls, or perhaps, I now think twice of the overly ripe,
overly over-ready red-green detailed laced box, the mascara made-

up face of an unaccounted for humid August evening of stark naked
purpose and partly undressed promise. Perhaps, now, I hide behind

the color of red tall ballroom dancing shoes, asked not to be removed.
Red soft silk, tender tights clinging un-wanting-ly. De-decorated lace,

leathery long black gloves that kept sliding down towards me. Eyes,
paralyzed by the hypnotic nature of not enough gin, the deception

of a reflection of two half-moons, full, nippled in waffled syrup, raw
honey circling a heat storm. Burning hot touching tips, lips melting

passionately into the unfaithfulness of our forgiveness as if maybe
tomorrow has nothing else to do but lick sweet flakes of forever out

of carefully crafted exit bullet wounds. The television was playing,
muting out the un-scandalous sounds of exotic pain spanked pleasure.

We didn't know, we could no longer hear the movie's dialogue. We
only imagined the stage play, *Desire* 1936, only guessed in the dark

what Marlene Dietrich was so taken aback by, so lustfully in love
with, so glamorously, wonderfully enjoying. Choice and chance in that

placid green painted room, that evening, pushed the whole world deep
into the small-ness of cracks between believe and not believe. New Year's

Eve, the rhyme of August nights. So the story goes like this: Some dark
brown handsome, handmade feelings felt the puzzle of white puzzle

pieces and placed, beautifully, each piece perfectly as almost perfect,
exactly where it should not be. Marlene's mirror, back-dropped, pretty,

in placid green, kept looking at us, glued, staring as if Berlin, herself,
was a burning theatre-night room watching the parts we play. Marie

Magdalene Dietrich as Lola Lola in *Blue Angel* 1930 slowly turning
a star-crossed night into a one night, all night, next morning newspaper

stand standing on a street corner without a name, collecting the last
quarters of a movie that kept on playing as we fell so unsoundly asleep.

SUCH IS THE LOVE STORY OF SALLY

(Sarah Hemings, 1773-1835)

They called her yellow children the yellow children
of Monticello. The shadowed yellow sound of lying
noise, yet quiet synonyms reveal such is the story of
Sally Hemings. Even now,

not all, but many, still, can't believe the sleeve of
Thomas Jefferson's pearl button war silk jacket, she
sewed in reverence as the never-
intended-to-be-announced Duchess of Monticello.

It was not the first time that Thomas Jefferson asked
her to dance. But first recorded, first in Paris. "May I
have this dance, Sally?"   A quiet question
that was not a question reflected
somewhat clear, somewhat obscure, the ancient symbolic

history of figs ripe in the hazel eyes of a slave girl called
Sally. Sally, his dear dead wife Martha's half-sister.
Sally, his oldest daughter, Martha's aunt. Sally, his dear

dead wife's late father's concubine's daughter. Sally,
the child of her sweet song singing mother, Helen.
Sally, the daughter of Virginia dirt and dust and lust.

Proper handles, proper size,
the shape of a plow, in his Garden Book, Jefferson

sketched, yet drew not upon the candor of
previous pages buried   book-shelved-deep

in the dark, fertile dirt fields of Monticello. Dashing
Miss Sally and their father,
Martha and Polly, the younger daughter, loved
beyond fault, whereas, inasmuch as they could not.

A dangerous decision of the heart, 1789. "May I ...?"
Thomas Jefferson's silence   seemed total.
He wrote careful letters to friends and enemies, careful
not to reveal his art of taste
for Sally's dark softness on moon-less Monticello nights.

The politics of a question mark marked in advance,
Thomas Jefferson's life. Drama upon the dramatics of
leaving footprints
without tracks, leaving shoe tracks without the impressions
of having visited Sally's small room at all.

Closed-curtain life left wide open. Words of severity,
compulsively controlled. Dream sung days. Slave-made
shutters of Monticello, propped open on purpose.

John Adams, the second president, tells the story of
Sally's beauty, having seen her walking in London city-
Rain, soaked in Virginia royalty. Sally Hemings, street-
stylish, Parisian clothes, strolling
beneath a pastel pink parasol, listening
to the promenading language of
rain beaten poetry, listening at a time in American history

that disallowed her black beauty to be beautiful. Still she
was more beautiful than any flower planted at Monticello.

Sally born a slave named Sarah Heming, 1773,
Charles City County, Virginia Colony. Sally's beauty,
that of a fruit tree. Sally, the shape of pear-sliced-
beauty sliced
between naked dark honesty and tragedy. Owl eyes

un-flinching, Virginia gentry looked down upon that which
was above their envying whispers, lamp light love,
the beautiful burning smell of.

Many of them heard, but could not hear Thomas' dear
dead Martha's harpsichord
reshaping the language of red roses and soft blowing breezes.
Between every season there is another name. Pointed words
bruise deep, but love knows not of defeat. Days of
village voice gentry came to call upon Sally as a scandal.

To be seen, no elaborate dance of denial graceful enough
to deny the classic story book beauty of Sally. Jefferson

never discussed that which he did discuss.
Monticello fire place mantle silent
as the burning smell of burning wood,
warming the voice of winter weather. Yet

Jefferson never wore a coat warm enough to reveal
the complete dance steps of why Sally's wardrobe
was packed for Paris. A dusty Virginia

day, 1787. Sally was 14. After 26 months, and a French tutor,
Sally returned speaking enough French to unfreeze
the frozen Seine some freezing Paris winter nights.

Big with child, greeted graciously by the dark side of
a slave shaped crescent moon.   Two days before
Christmas Eve, 1789, the Virginia sun forgot to forget,
forgot to forgive whispering voices of Virginia gentry.

Thunder married the maelstroms of politics, echoing
seamlessly, endlessly across unplowed fields of aristocratic
white folk weeds asking,

"Why have you not married a worthy woman
of your own complexion?" Sally, big with child. They all
knew, but none dare imagine   the resemblance,

striking.   Tom, a baby boy, Sally's first of six
yellow children, white enough to pass for white. So they
blended out into the music of far reaching towns,

taking full unnoticed-public notice of   passing
glances and circumstances of. Therefore, thereafter,
they lived a white life
and died as the President's yellow children.

No one knows why as did the breeze not carve
into barks of Monticello trees "Tom Loves Sally." But
whispering winds   singing pine straw songs

knew the soft steps of   secrets were not secret at all.
They knew, yes, yet none dare say, none dare see
the common consequences of a love story, center stage,

the Camelot of Monticello. A Shakespeare tragedy,
jealousy in the hills of   Virginia gentry. They
called Sally "concubine."
Too beautiful to be or not to be, the tragedy of Sally.

Between every season ... Nothing good comes out of
nothing good. Every direction plotted to dismantle
that which could not be dismantled, Jefferson's love
of listening to lyrics
of reticent rain beat upon the roof over Sally's head.

Chained to the never square corners of circumstance,
Jefferson's silence seemed total, a surveyor's intent.

Time tells, only, the story of a two term President. Time
tells, only, the story of Meriwether Lewis and Clark
looking for the Pacific side of the State of Louisiana. Yet
time, I guess,
forgot, only, the story of Sally, the First Lady of Monticello.

So now with the ease of looking at a beautiful view, look
now, please,
into the eyes of Thomas Jefferson, a Memorial situated
on the Tidal Basin among
flowering Japanese cherry trees still blowing breezes

of slave-made days.   Many dare see the bronze
sculptured, naked nature of forgetting to remember Sally,
sculpted upon marble,
monumental blue. Sally,
sculpted in years of dried red rose petals dried between
the pages of Jefferson's Garden Book. Look,
no, don't look now,
wait, now look.
Focus, no need.
Camera lens of honesty focus automatically. Any frame
composed
composes beautiful the composition of Sally's song. Snap
a shot, take a picture.
Close shutter speed quick as the speed of no sound at all.

STILL LIFE

Covid on Canvas, Spring 2020

Six feet deep translated into six feet apart, the complete, sad
design of sad social distance. Every
eye-color gazed to the sanitized floor of a local grocery store.
A spaced-out cross mark tells us to, "Stand Here"   and wait
and watch cans of Lysol disinfectant *scan* them-selves as if
the spray, itself, knows we won't go home   without it.

We acrylicize the sad silence of weekdays
when Cleaning Aisle shelves were   stocked full. The next
available self-checkout register,   we wait. Rush hour
is more than an hour. We've learned to sneeze inside-out, cough
upside down.   Simple Dawn soap suds, we now worship.
Even "bad" mannerism, we sanitize through the voices of masks.

No Hugs Allowed haunts even the clothes we wear
these depleted days. One summer that never begins.   We wait.
We have learned the dance
of being too close to forgetting to stay calm, stay stable, stay
at home, work from home, clock-in, clock-out on kitchen-time.
We never knew,
exactly, the number of channels on cable TV, never knew,
exactly, the number of hours in a stay-home day.   But now,
we do.
We've learned to home-school our children,
pre-school
to high school by ringing an 8 o'clock AM homeroom bell.

Laptops on kitchen tables teach science and mathematics,
ABCs and XYZs

What we've learned,
learns us to Zoom, virtually, from every room.
We, now, calculate the square footage of no empty space
left to paint.
We have learned to open public doors without hands,
greet friends with fist-bumps. We paint disappointments
with calendar squares
of F2F appointment times with better days. Our kids,
we cherish their paint-by-number ways these
be-careful, slow turning days. We've not flown for months
of airlines afraid to fly. We've lived

for months in towns of restaurants reluctant
to remember to open their family friendly arms. The bar
next door may never open again. Just yesterday, Starline
Books, the mom and pop bookstore where my daughter worked
before college, decided
to close for good and for bad. Packing up boxes of books,
breaking down boxes of already broken hearts, the weight
of these days! Still we rise
just as Maya Angelou told us to so,
again, just before she died.

And as Spring 2020 folded, then
faded into early Fall school days, *smiling at and to everyone*
we meet as we go on our, now, any-time-of-day walks
has magically,

organically (all natural ingredients) become
the new mental health drug of choice. And
on neighborhood walks, we have learned our neighbors' names,
where they work,
where they're from,
how long they've lived here.
We, now, know more than the styles and colors of the cars
they drive past our homes. And

in this season of street protest for social justice, we have learned
that Black Lives Matter
has never been painted onto the American landscape except
during the prosperous economic times of slavery. We know
the Clorox bleach of hesitation,
isolation cannot wash that stain off of our hands. And

in these no-spring-training baseball days of double play doubt,
days of so many among us striking out,
first pitch, we have carefully
swung for fences of flat, acrylic, interior paint. We've fallen
in love with the small corners between
remembering and forgetting to love. We've been drafted. We're

soldiers in a war of many fronts: global warming, melting job
rates, racial unrest, political up-side-down-ness,
tornado alley expanding, named hurricanes running out of names,
white supremacy rewriting the Civil War,
raging floods, raging Red rhetoric,
raging wildfires

in California. Raging, a pandemic the size of everything
we don't want to know. And

as the world turns to welcome winter, we still wear
the Bermuda Triangle
shorts of summer studio light.
Faith in our front and back pockets next to cell phones
that have deleted the *departed,* six feet deep.   Six feet apart
gait, straight into wherever we walk.   Still life,   we wait
for the full harvest moon of sweet nights remembered.
We have learned to paint the patience of fruit trees.

BLUES DISGUISED AS JAZZ

for the King of Water Street, 1930-1972

In this sleepy town still asleep
where Fish House Street is called
by the name of Wet Water Street,
my father proclaimed himself
King of everything but. Every day
of his short life, day light, fish box
jazz
cornered his imagination into believing
the catch of the day
really was caught that day.
But on the fish house docks, wet with
the fish sweat juice of everyday,
Negro boy life, water rushed in
jazz
to meet the mornings of Cape Fear,
scaring everyone in that wet
water world but my father.
Never was he afraid of the hateful,
watered down words,
cascading
blues
up and down from the stale, white
voices of proper white-fish-truck-
driving, white proper conduct.

Jazz,
He, my father, drove his fish truck
without permission to please
my mother, "the man," or the worth
of a wet water raced-up world
curled up at the edge of
blues
Carolina hurricane season.
No reason ever
given to the lack of
jazz
forgiveness. But he, my father never
forgot or
forgave the drinking water in water fountains
for not allowing him
to drink, to think of himself as anything but
blues,
a Negro boy with no
money, to speak or not speak of,
in his khaki pants pocket.
No British-made Windsor tied necktie to
jazz
dress-up his
blues.
My father, forsaken
by fish and grits for breakfast.
A life of nothing left to remember but his
white boy white

white shirt white
white as the white
white Oxford shirt white
gift Grandmamma gave to me when I graduated
from high school.
But my father, the blue jazz King of Wet Water Street
would be dead and gone by then.

THE THINGS THEY CARRIED

(Crisco Martinez' 1950-1969)

Crisco died with his soldier in his hand.
That's right, he was taking a piss   and
a Vietcong sniper boy picked him   off
long distance.

The morning was one of those mornings
when everyone felt safe, as safe as we could
feel in the bush.   It was a scene, perhaps,
from a war movie. The year of our lord, 1969.

Neil Armstrong was still walking on the moon.
We were walking towards daybreak, a platoon
of eighteen boys in loose rank.

The report we got said "The area ain't hot."
So we relaxed and walked slow and talked low
about girls back home.

Crisco's girl was Susan, a buxom blonde
he said he met somewhere in California.
Said she was prettier than the picture
he carried like a god in his army shirt pocket.
Said they were going to be married
when his tour of duty was over.

It was a good day to be outside.
There was a breeze, nice and cool and easy

as a Sunday morning in low country SC.
We were stepping from the shade into the bright sunlight.

We'd just smoked a joint, shoe-laced with heroin.
We were floating on seasick waves and that white
horse was starting to kick like a Texas rodeo.
We were not paying attention. The birds were singing

The air smelled fresh.   The sky was chamber music
and was clear.   It was not a morning for war movies.

We were walking in loose rank and laughing
and talking about girls back home.
We were drifting.   It wasn't stove-top hot.
There was a breeze, nice and cool and easy.

The banyan trees were movie props, a Hollywood
of slow dancing leaves.   The joint was good.
That white horse was kicking.
We were not paying attention.
We were joking and talking about girls back home.
Crisco was going to be married.

The sky was chamber music and was clear.
The birds were singing.
It was hot.
There was a breeze.
It was a good day for a white wedding.
And all the best men were standing right there
watching the rice of unbleached rain   fall.

THE SOUNDS OF SUMMER (BASEBALL CARDS)

Somebody told somebody that everybody told
Neil Armstrong to not even bother stepping foot
on the Negro side of the moon.   June, August
and July, three segregated summertime sisters
agreed, weather-wise. The year of our lord, 1969
was a color-line   shaped like   no shape at all.

It occurs to me now that before I left home,
hitchhiking, at age 16,   I did not know
that some things continue to go missing long after
they are found, and I didn't realize that the physics
of throwing a baseball explains   every ounce of
racial tension in America. But I won't talk about that
now. Now, I want to talk about love.   As a kid, I fell
in love with the sounds of
the names of   baseball players:
Henry Louis "Hank" Aaron, Roger Eugene Maris,
Edward Charles "Whitey" Ford, Willie Mays, Willie
McCovey, Maury Wills, Billy Williams, Ernie Banks
and Stanley Frank Musial, the St. Louis music man.

And I can still hear the names,   baseball games
between the Temptations, the Supremes, the 4 Tops,
Motown songs   on Grandmama's transistor radio.

"Crack," the sound of a baseball kissing the sweet spot
of a baseball bat. "That ball's outta here," the always white
announcer would yell towards the Colored sport section

of my yellowed newspaper wallpapered room. And what
about the other pages in the other yellowed corners of
my unheard short radio story?   And what about
that white boy,   classmate in every class that year?
He'd never seen a "stolen base" like me. I didn't know
I was supposed to knock him out.   I didn't know
I was a nigger until   he called me   "Nigger"

deep in the very bottom of the 9th.   Me at the plate,
"crack," a walk off (case closed) home run, dead center,
solid between the hazel-blue color of   two blue eyes.

The Pender County Board of Education didn't see it
that way in base-hit terminology. Me, expelled completely
from the school system for life   for being the "nigger"
I did not know I was until ...

Still, so be it, anyway and yes,   I know I was
raised in a small, white town of three white Jesuses,
Baptist,   Presbyterian   and Methodist,
none of which I liked much or loved the way I
loved potato salad, fried chicken and collard greens,
picnic-style-served   after Negro church services
on Sunday, summer afternoons   in the yard of
a church without a denomination. But the choir could
sing a stairway to Heaven and part way back if you
decided to get off along the way.   Each of

the three white Jesuses had nice white churches with
tall steeples and   summer league baseball teams,
but I never asked to pray or play.   Perhaps

I knew way back then, if water could be segregated,
"strike zones"   could be tailor made not to fit
a Black baseball boy growing up   in White Town.

Grandmama must've thrown my baseball cards
in the trash the day I left, the day the Board of
Pender County Education decided I didn't need any
more education. Years

later, Grandmama couldn't remember, but I still
remember the magic. Yes, even now on some lazy
weather summer days, I'm eleven years old again,
listening lightly,   my voice   opening a pack of
baseball cards, the sounds of summer.   Me, side-
stepping up and down a dirt country road,
almost swallowing the afternoon,   the chew of
stale, hard baseball card chewing gum
stuck to the bottom of somebody else's shoes, my
clean-up-batter blues.

And then, somehow, I find what I never did lose,
piano music playing clouds across a Carolina blue
sky, reminding me   quite beautifully
as I call out the sounds   of the names I loved:
Rico Petrocelli, Jose Santiago,
Louis Aparicio,
Bill Mazeroski,   Dizzy Dean and Dizzy Trout,
Roberto Clemente   and Tony Conigliaro.

BREAKFAST IN AMERICA

Brown vs the Board of My Education

I never did eat lunch-bucket peanut butter
sandwiches for school lunch from the same
lunch bucket,
in the same dead-mud peanut butter field
where my father was born. But I know
my father's story better than my father did.

Beside a riverboat sign in between unsacred
ugly red colors of ugly
Cape Fear red River water, my father died.
Where
the Wilmington [Black] Massacre of 1898 still
breezes over the streets 365 nigger-nights a year,
my father lived.   No Negroes Allowed
stamped in the labels of my father's shirts could
not be laundered out.

From tragic doubt, I came out into a color-by-
numbers, divided world.
My name is my father's namesake, Earl the 2nd.
My father was the Earl of Everything.
He did not pay attention. I am the Earl of Nothing.
I have learned to see what my father could not.

Like Pablo Picasso, I know I must have been
born dead
in the middle of my father's poverty. The face

of my father, I came out of my mother's womb
begging forgiveness for that which I did not do.

Everyday and everything in my Black growing-up
life was a magic miracle. I've lived the strange
life of a Negro paperboy poet without pencil or pen,
so I paint abstract artificiality in Black and white
coloring books, white looks and stares of invisibility.

My father worked on fish house docks. I never did,
but my mind jumps, these days, like the history of
Cape Fear River catfish   reciting
essential lessons for Negroes in my hometown, 1898,
a night when white supremacists
caused the Cape Fear to run red with Negro blood.

Growing up, street science poor in housing projects,
my father's hesitations fashioned me not to believe
in the principles of Einstein.
E never did = mc^2.   Everything in projects life
is beyond the realities of Relativity. Light travels
slower than the speed of sound in Blacklifeville.

The pocket knife my father carried, dull,
in his pocket, I now carry in mine. It's hard
to be sharp when ordinary days design
you to be blunt. But dull eventually cuts.

Growing up, dreams of becoming, I had
no need for them.
I attended schools that didn't teach Black

children the language of misaligned stars
and the beauty of constructing your own
constellations. Perseverance is a forced virtue.

Never missed a single day of school, never
turned in one assignment late, never
got a grade in the mathematics of No
Name in the Street
that didn't make Miss Jones, Miss Brown
and Mr. McGee proud of me and the way
I see around corners my father could not.

A good student, not perfect, I never tried to be.
How could any of us be in our under-funded,
run-down into the ground, ugly school that,
on white-people-purpose, did not want to know
the science of my name.

Every geography book I studied located Africa
behind the map. Every biology book I dissected
already had a white boy or white girl's name
written in a space designed to be the first thing
Black boys and Black girls see when Black boys
and Black girls open the first page of American
History. So, no place for us, no place for me
to write my name.

Street life in Blacklifeville is a hard teacher
and she teaches the science of the arithmetic of
Nothing from Nothing leaves
Nothing for you to learn

but what the design of America designed you
to learn. So you learn early on
how to get locked up in jail, behave well, get out
early so you can go back soon.

Prison systems in America are built to be filled
to Negro capacity. It's a business, an Investment,
slave auction block/Stock Market
Niggers   on Wall Street, a lucrative incentive.

Growing up, every family I knew
had at least one family member in prison. All
three of the Salter brothers were locked up
at the same time in the same system. They

learned and got caught. I learned and did not.

I learned to tie a square knot with square rope.
I learned how to steal a grape off of a grapefruit tree,
I learned how to holdup Jesse James and Billy
and walk away
with a complete stereo system
from Sears and Roebuck Department Store
with the cashier and the clerk saying
"Thank you for shopping at Sears, you come
back now, you hear"   I heard.

Good-bad habits grow in the bushes of housing
projects
where hovering police sanctioned helicopters
drop "white" drug supplies onto Black People Street.

I know how the smell of heroin
melts in a metal Coca Cola glass-bottle cap.
I know how matches burn down whole cities
when you don't *Close Cover Before Striking*

three times   out. My father struck out,
he dropped out of school in the sixth grade.

My father stayed in the batter's box, standing
at a plate all of his short-stop life
without a homerun pitch with any intentions
of coming across his plate. I stepped out of
the box so I could see the left field fence of
possibility.   When the wind blows nothing

good your way every day, you learn the story
of improvisational baseball spin. In Blacklifeville
school is always
in session
You learn to harness the smallness of tiny things.
You learn to make the no-good taste good.
You learn to walk like money when you are broke.
You learn to talk with luck like a fake gold tooth.
You learn to improvise with no surprise.
You learn to dance the dance of indecision.
You know death in the streets by heart.
You know the policeman is a trigger-nigger poet.
You know there's no line between justice and "Just us".
You learn to love the smell of fish and grits

served in restaurants, cafes, bars and grills of No-
Colored-People-Allowed   defect. You learn, you
learn, you learn   what the history of "No
Space for You" anywhere   teaches you to learn:

Breakfast in America taught me to eat left-handed.

CLOCKWORK BACK, THE CONFEDERACY OF FENCES

If you want to know how Miss America became America
the Beautiful, land of the free, don't ask me, ask Demark

Vesey, born in 1767 in Saint Thomas, hanged on July 2nd
1822 in Charleston, South Carolina for preaching truth.

For reasons, officially stated unknown. The moon, shaped
like a gun that day in history just like yesterday in history,

the day GRAY, they took down the Confederate Battle Flag.
Slow to fall upon the grounds of the town of James "Strom"

Thurmond's City. The history of two weeks ago is too long
of a way to go, so somebody, anybody walked into Demark

Vesey's AME church and shot Demark Vesey 9 more times,
point blank, in the face. Among the dead faces, propped up

on the face of a dark skinned, today-yesterday, modern day
poster Harriet Tubman and Sojourner Truth, Nat Turner

and Gabriel Prosser and David Walker's *Appeal* to reveal
what tends, always, to be left out of our history, the truth of

and about the Confederate Battle Flag history of heritage
and hate, beyond too late to debate, but since we are talking

about *Truth and Consequences*, and such, let's look closely at the economic impact of walls, fences and Confederate flags,

GRAY, stiff and dead, red, white and broken-up blue glass. Slavery in America was/is an exact science designed, and then

implemented in or about 1623 to make America beautiful. A little white baby boy, the youngest country in the world

in 1776, become the richest country in the world a century or so later, give or take a "few" boat loads of curious cargo,

the Negro. And it worked terribly beautiful, the scientific experiment, it worked beautifully like clockwork black, not

orange. Free labor, the economic stimulus package of... Don't ask me, ask J. Paul Getty and Andrew Carnegie.

So, now the question becomes one of "what." What is America's net-gain-contribution put forth on the 4th of

July by the people America the Beautiful referred to as such and such, Niggers-Negro-African cargo. HANDLE

with NO CARE. The intent meant only for "Darwinism" to survive, to arrive alive. How many didn't make the trip?

Perhaps GRAY wants not to ... Trans-Atlantic partnership with one partner landing in CharlesTown, South Carolina,

beautiful Port City, America. Negro cargo-stated inventory:
uncountable "This one has good teeth, this one has a good...

Black chaos calculations, exact as inexact, unfurled slowly
as 13 stars that hate me and bars of already-sold-gold that

tell and told lies. Low and behold, slavery. Built on the backs
of blacks, America the Beautiful is ugly. Sojourner's Truth.

The African Methodist Episcopal Church of Charleston,
South Carolina founded by Demark Vesey, burned down

to the ground in 1822. The African American Episcopal
Church of Charleston, South Carolina re-mass murdered

again during prayer meeting on Wednesday night, June 17th
2015, approximately 9:05 p.m. Daylight Savings Time. Motive,

heritage and hate. It's too late to take the flag down. But if you
ask me, which you vehemently refuse to do, I will tell to you

Sojourner's Truth. Don't take the rebel flag down, put it up.
Let it fly, unfurl over the "Republican Side" of the Capitol

Building side of the Un-United States of America the Beautiful
ugly side. I'll tell you the truth, that is if you want to know why

the 1963, 16th Street Baptist Church of Birmingham, Alabama
still burns. Smell the smoke, the still fresh char of burnt flesh.

4 little black school girls   studying the Bible   Sunday school
Addie Mae,
Cynthia,
Carole and
Denise.   15 sticks of   KKK   dynamite

attached to a timing device beneath the front steps of the 16th
Street Baptist Church of Birmingham, Alabama. Why, still,

does the Confederate Battle flag of This-Town, South Carolina
unfurl so proudly, but only to the static movement of a neo-new

nigger-Negro blown wind that's been dead for years now? Don't
ask me, don't ask me, please don't ask me, ask Demark Vesey.

THE HALF LIFE OF CHOCOLATE

(Revisiting the imagined-now voice
of my great-great grandmother, Miss Carolina Brown)

I'm 87 years old, if I live to see tomorrow morning's sun,
I'll be 88 and still counting from 1865 to nowhere – to stop,

on a regular basis, Confederate gray pickup trucks, waving
rebel flags, a sight that never did, much, bother me. You see,

I was born in the bright sun on the farm-life sad outskirts of
Mr. Charles Town, South Carolina on a little piece of pitiful

land my father and his father before him sharecropped until
"bad" back-taxes broke Daddy's back and Daddy's heart,

but not father's soul. On the Sunday I came into this world,
a nice, white country doctor working part-time, sometime,

at a Colored hospital tied thirteen stars and two chocolate
candy bars, twisted tight, around my neck and sent me and

Mama back home. Heritage and hate, since then, ungracefully
I have worn and worn, natural as a lamb's wool (like Jesus's

hair, Mamma said) winter coats in winter or a light cotton,
summer, church skirt in August. August straight through

July knows as God knows my dark skin is admired far more
than it is hated, but secrets are kept top-silent for a reason.

Treason seasons of moonshine love, the relationship between
Thomas and Sally, between boundaries and beauty, the sweet

texture of bitter chocolate. Ancestors who built plantations
here are "My people." They planted and picked ten million

bales of cotton, planted and picked a billion cups of Low
Country rice. Then wider than white, wild white brims of

the plantation white hat wearers sold their nigger-harvest
for billions in dollar bill signs. But, my ancestors were paid,

each chocolate one of them given two or three thin slices of
thin-love bacon per square acre and a dead-deal mule deal.

The arithmetic of America wants not to know more, the score.
Secrets are kept top-silent-secret for a reason, but the science

of storytelling tells the children the half-life of chocolate is short.
Colored people in America live half in shadow, half on Sunshine

Street. Chocolate melts so quickly in fields of summer, coastal
South Carolina heat. I'm 87 years old. When I was young, I was

a school teacher. I taught arithmetic, so I know how to count
Confederate bumper stickers on the bumpers of "Republican"

colored cars and deer-hunting pickup trucks and I have seen
my share of Klansmen, women, and cute little children march

to the beat and banner of heritage and hate. I cannot count how
many white plate fine China dishes I have washed in too many

White House-hold kitchens to count. I even met the late Senator
"Mr." James Strom Thurmond years before the people forgot

they knew his real history was not his real history at all. Y'all
think it's a grand thing to take down the Confederate flag flying

over Columbia, the esteemed capitol of the Great Slave State of
South Carolina and I suppose it is, but a flag pole has no feelings

that I know of, and the wind that blows the unfurled does not
care if it shares the Carolina Confederate gray-blue sky with

Confederate bluebirds, redbirds or not. The sky does not ask
why. What y'all should do is leave the Confederate Battle flag

up,
furling
and unfurling
its crossed out honor,
its crossed out breeze

and ease the Stars and Bars,
the Confederate Battle flag
down
from around
my neck. It's hard to choke a flag pole to death.

THE WEIGHT OF NOT ANSWERING

for the spaces in Sarah

Don't look now, I, too, am fading into the noise of
these ugly named streets that decided not to answer
the one question Sarah couldn't bring herself to pose
like a photograph taken   when we were young,

when we were in high school glee club   singing
dancing-in-the-rain-Gene Kelly songs and did not
know the yellow dress she wore,
she would still be wearing so many "partly cloudy"
afternoons after   the morning after.

Of course, he didn't know her name was Sarah,
didn't know she was Sagittarius, didn't know she
turned 23 the last day of last November and just
less than 6 months ago, she'd moved down here
from Cambridge,   didn't know she waited
tabled with her Harvard art degree. And of course,
he didn't know the landscape of   Sarah's smile.

But, somehow, he knew her apartment number, 207,
knew she mostly worked night shift,   knew she
always couldn't find her door key,   knew she came
home, always, alone and late and, seemingly, too tired
to sleep.   The bedroom lamplight was a Tiffany
of confused numbness. He knew low balconies don't
like ladders.   And somehow, he knew
Sarah's second story window felt safe   enough

in her "up and coming" neighborhood to be left cracked
open on no breeze blowing across the wee hour thin-
ness of the Sarah's futon, made in Sweden. Foreign-

currency-recounted mornings later, she didn't mean to
cry, but city bus-riders eyes gave to her no choice, so
she wandered wet streets with no raincoat. She decided
to edit-out, completely, the morning rush of wee hours.

The afternoon was silent as a silent motion picture
show. She loved, always has, rain, rain, the sound of
falling water falling in love with falling water.
But now, futon fitted sheets of ... does not remember
Sarah's name, and the thunder, inaudible.

7 weeks, 2 days later, the space between blades of grass,
a Thursday morning that knows the unknowns are still
empty in crowded, wet streets. Wearing the same yellow
dress, she's sitting in a waiting room in a floral print chair
that struggles to smell of flowers. She is waiting, listening
to elevator music, elevator music that seems not
to know that there is only one story angled

between the pages of every self-help-movie-star magazine
on every coffee table in the world of rooms designed
for women to just wait and wait and wait. Sarah is
waiting, pondering who decides when to put what where.

Monet, Cezanne, Pissarro, Vincent, waiting room walls
are all the same, framed Impressionists looking at you.

Sarah is waiting, watching a waiting room clock forget,
holding, tightly, my hand with both of hers,   waiting,
trying to remember the sound of someone, anyone calling
her name, Sarah.   Pressing the pleats of a yellow dress
with no pleats, crossing and uncrossing her legs, waiting.

And then   she's smiling, because she just caught
a glimpse of herself   watching a Vincent Van Gogh
yellow sun roll right out of   the waiting room window.

THE OTHER COLOR OF RAINWATER

The George Perry Floyd Story

Burning streets and ugly-news times have undone my eyes
again.   Somewhere, at this moment,
I hear Nina Simone   singing to a night sky full of stars,
"I wish I knew what it feels like to be free." "I wish, I wish
I knew what it feels like to be free." A broken record in stereo,

a pre-test, post-test   protest testing the endurance of ugly,
evil blue tinted smoke   emanating, quite brilliantly
from the eyes of a   yellow haired   Labrador Deceiver,
dog-housed in New York City,   a Tower of Babbling
continuously foolish, incomprehensible   rapicities of lies
disguised to divide the design   of diversity dancing in streets
around the world.

Black Lives Matter, London, Paris, Copenhagen. Black Lives
Matter,   Madrid, Brazil, Bangkok, Tokyo, Berlin, Toronto,
Black Lives Matter,   Seoul City, South Korea
Black Lives Matter   Sir Charlestown, South Carolina.
Black Lives Matter, Sugar Ditch, Mississippi, Alabama, Georgia.
Tennessee.   Fox News fox hounds, overfed.
Dead red state political stance can't figure out the dance of wolves.
James Brown   "Say it loud, I'm Black and I'm proud"
loud speaking   everywhere   at the same time.

George Floyd's car radio was still playing when he died
with a white   police   man's   black boot   substituting
as a lynch mob noose. Too loose,   the interpretation of

sparks in a nation's eyes watching the funeral-dead eyes of
George Floyd on a dead-hot   afternoon
in Houston, Texas, Anywhere.   Answers in America,

these days, tend to be framed as Donald ducking questions
without question marks. Try these 4 questions on for size,
see if they fit the size of   your 72 inch wide flat screen.

What white "police special" color   was that police van
that transported Freddie Gray all the way   to his grave?

How old was 17-year-old Trayvon Martin when he walked
out of that inconvenient   -convenient store?

What was Emmett Till's mother's   maiden name?

How long is 8 minutes and 46 seconds   of Critical Race Theory
that America wants not   to learn to count the economic
arithmetic of slavery or   the biological   psycho   logics of
remembering why   Jim Crowism wasn't written in the book.
Now you just take a look:
Sitting there in the back seat of a Montgomery, Alabama City bus,
Rosa Parks   couldn't breathe.
Fannie Lou Hamer   couldn't breathe.
Harriet Tubman   couldn't breathe.
Ida B. Wells   couldn't breathe.
Mary Church Terrell   couldn't breathe.
Brown vs The Board of Negro Education still can't breathe.
And
what about that black boot? Was it polished, spit shined?
What about that black boot?   It is same black boot.

It is the history of being a Negro in America,
just a different shoe size purchased from a different whitefront
storefront on a different Black Friday afternoon.

George Floyd called his mama's name. Mama, I can't breathe
George Floyd, 46 years old, DOA Dead On Arrival
exactly 46 years, 7 months and 11 days before he died.
Obituary:
George Perry Floyd Jr. (Oct. 14, 1973-May 25, 2020),
a good son, a loving father, a beloved brother, reduced,
now to the broken neck of a sunflower, a sunflower
mis-watered, mistreated, mis-irrigated for 46 years
in ghetto-gardens of dirty, unthinkable, undrinkable
Flint, Michigan, weathered rainwater. George Perry
Floyd Jr. was not designed to know how to breathe in,
now breathe out in America.

The day he died, African drums rained and rained
and rained as far back in history as the Alex Haley's *Roots*
of every African American family tree. We ..., me.

As the body of George Floyd Jr. was being lowered back
into the earth Nina Simone's voice was, still, spinning
an American-made turntable, a broken, long-playing record,

Mississippi god damn, Mississippi god damn,
A broken record in stereo
Mississippi god damn, Mississippi god damn.
"I wish I knew what it feels like to be free."
Mississippi god damn, Mississippi god damn.

IN WHICH LANGUAGE DO I KEEP SILENT

for a woman I saw dancing

I know that if a number is raised to the 1st power,
the exponent   is usually not written. I know
that the absolute value of a number is that number
without a sign. Without a sign, there is no way to tell
who I am.   I will not give any indications.

I know that the angular velocity of your movement
is too beautiful to name and I've come to recognize
you as a dancer in lines of my own poetry.
It's a funny thing how books can be read upside down
and maps get us most lost.   I know this
from the experience of waiting for the moon to sing.

Lately, I find myself looking at maps, measuring
the distance between   little big town music
and cities.
1 inch = 25 miles, 1/25th of 1 inch = 1 mile.
Small places, represented as pencil dots. I question
the mathematics of it all.   My whole numbers

have become fractions on a November calendar.
I've learned to count parts of each square. I know
what it's like to have nothing   but time.

The night I first saw you dance between rivers,
I followed the softness
of your steps across the floor, across the studio,

every spin taken into consideration, every jump.
I know
the shortest distance between us is a straight line.

I want to leap with you but not tonight
because when I divide the time of day into the time
I have known you,
multiplied by the number of times you've crossed
my mind lately,
the answer is way too early to tell what I'm feeling.
I know the wrong answer is not always wrong.

Do you know how to tango? Would you teach me
to dance to
the unexplained, deliberate as the unexplored dances
to the patterns of treasure maps.
Would you teach me to close my eyes when I kiss?

I know the co-efficient of *A* to the second power is 1.
I know what it feels like
to be alone in a blue room too many nights in a row.

I know how to fly without wings.
If you were a jet airliner traveling at 7.50 km while
gaining altitude at a constant rate, if you traveled
between points 5.80 km apart, what is the gain
in altitude? I would figure it out and meet you
at the vertex. I know the Pythagorean Theorem.

I know some mornings my dreams lie to me
to make me feel better.

I laugh, trying to figure out the ones I now have.
I am not saying
I dream about you. I'm saying you are in my dreams
and most often I wake up falling. I know the distance
I fall = ½ times the time squared it takes me to fall.

According to Atlas and road maps,   my silence
is 1 mile away from you in either direction I decide to
go or not go.   I know that speed = distance divide by
the time I sit here and wait. I know exactly how long
it should take if I were to measure your gaze in either
of the two languages I now speak.

I light myself another cigarette. I don't say a thing,
I ponder   the velocity of silence.

MILES DAVIS PLAYS TRUMPET AT THE FUNERAL OF MALCOLM X

I could begin by telling you he rode two horses
at once   without falling off only to fall face first
between   the dark street night legs of the Nation
of Islam.

I could tell you that this is Harlem in the year
of our Lord,   1965 and Malcolm is still standing
there   next to that dying room window,   peeking
out through a rifle and a scope,   looking,   looking
into the face of   dead   pan   dead   hope.

I could tell you why   damn near every one of us
aces   locked up   in this here place is black   as a deck
of playing card spades.   I ain't wearing no dark shades

I could tell you a lot of things,   I could tell you
a lot of stuff, but I won't   not just yet.

What I will tell you is this: Today is Sunday.
Sunday is nigger-fried chicken day.   Sunday
is movie day   here inside   of   Angola Rodeo
Louisiana State Prison,   the largest maximum-security
prison in   the United States of America. Believe it
or not,   there is   and there are   damn near 6,300
photographs of me   locked up in here. Yes, and just now

in-between NFL football games,   we're watching

a John Wayne picture show in slow motion black
and white, 16mm. Outside, though we can barely
hear it, we know it is refried-freeze-raining
a murder of crows.

Inside this place is a storm brewing in a killingly
kind coffee pot, percolating so death is no
stranger when he comes quiet as a movie night
whisper in a movie dark room, "Malcolm X is dead."

I cannot begin to describe the smell of fear in here
in a cup of hot coffee too black to drink, to think spilling
onto my lap, spilling
onto the front page of every newspaper
locked into newspaper boxes
on every street corner
in the Black United States of America.

Here's a dime. Get your own white slanted pages of
10 slant-face lies. I know it as it was.
Malcolm X was standing on stage in Harlem,
giving a speech.
Then Malcolm X fell onto a stage in Harlem,
giving a speech.
Then Malcolm X bled all over a stage in Harlem,
giving a speech.
Then Malcolm X died like a dog in the streets of Harlem,
giving a speech.

Apparently, according to us in here who look
exactly black like me, the Nation of Islam did

not love Malcolm as much as Malcolm loved us.

Now Malcolm X no more than an Alex Haley comic book
Superman. Look at me, I am a comic. Laugh.

It's a funny thing how things happen just like
in the movies, just like James Dean and Steve McQueen,
just like Errol Flynn, just like Tyrone. And if you
want to look at it in a Negro way, just like
Sydney Poitier. Just like me. Yes,
just like me. I've been locked up in here 3 years, 17
days and 9 hours. Sometimes at night, I turn out
the lights and dream backwards between these bars
and stripes and stars, always movie stars.

But this ain't no movie house popcorn
picture show sticking to the floor. It's blood
that makes a wedding rose red enough
to decorate the dead.

In here, most days, most things go wherever they go
without being said.
Outside the rain has stopped, but a murder of crows
don't care to know. They hovering over the kill.

The fried chicken is gone. What did you expect?
The movie, too, now is over and yes, John Wayne
got the girl, as he always does. Did you think he wouldn't?
I didn't.

Drinking cold coffee, smoking my cigarettes down
to the very end, I am the only one left, sitting here
in the middle of a now dead, quiet, sold-out show.

I am sweating police night-stick bullets, staring
at Minister Malcolm laid out
in the Negro stately -coffin manner of dead Negro royalty.

Somewhere, somehow, someway, a trumpet begins
to blow, softly at first, then slow. I turn to see the image
of a man blacker than me
leaning back into a corner blacker than he.

Miles Dewey Davis slow- reaching up to meet "Stella by Starlight,"
Miles Dewey Davis stretching all the way out "Sketches of Spain,
Miles Dewey Davis re-birthing the "Birth of the Cool."
Miles Dewey Davis laying down on top of "Someday
My Prince Will Come."

AND I THOUGHT ABOUT ...

Excuse me mister, but is you ah, ah, ah, nigger?
Excuse me sir, but is you ...?

Deflected, covered carefully, thoughts, my thoughts,
shifting shop-talk-walk, waking thoughts,

a crossed-stitched quilt of naked words,
blanketing
too warm for this kind of warm weather
silence
impending.   Excuse me sir, but ... ?

A little, sweet, kind-face white boy, whiter than
poor white trash,
sitting in the red bottomed backseat of
sad ugly love,
sitting respectfully up in

a Bi-Lo grocery shopping cart. asking
kindly of
me,
a kindergarten question.

Excuse me sir, but is you...?

And then there was a freeze, a frozen
lingering drop dead

right-where-you-are-right-now
silence,

a symphonic concert hall cacophony of
silence,

the history of the Negro in America to date
silence,

the psychology of James (Jimbo) Crow
silence,

the geography of a slave-trade wind selling
silence,

embraced, erased by the velocity of
silence,

the philosophy, psychology of it all —
silence

pushing past, into, kindly, explosive static
silence

kept silent by default,
my Tuesday afternoon, grocery store, Negro
silence.

Excuse me sir, but is you ah, ah…?

Then a metronome,
a swinging police night nigger night stick,
back and forth,
back and forth
back and forth
fly-fish fishing silence,

the science of dancing
to "just us" justice. Black
work hands picking "white"
cotton patches of silence.

Black souls working roots
like a voodoo doctor,
back and forth,
back and forth,
here and there
across unjust years and unjust weeks of
ugly sad love
silence.

Cold running ice water sweat silence.

Excuse me mister, but is you ah [black] nigger?

A beautiful, little blue eyed, white boy,
innocent
as his skinny white arms gesturing
pure, poor,
white naivete.

Innocent skinny white legs dangling,
honest as
honesty
from the back seat of a Bi-Lo grocery
shopping cart,

a Bi-Lo shopping cart that tells,
without, with no hesitation,
its annoying wobbly wheel noise

to any and everyone willing to listen
and not listen to the grocery shopping world
as it rolls
up and down
up and down
up and down
grocery store aisles. You know
the noise of that kind
of grocery cart by heart.

I know you do, don't you?

A grocery cart that has, let's say,
three good wheels
and one wheel
that leans too far into its own rolling
grocery store life,

a kind and simple grocery cart
that has momentarily stopped

squeaking, now peeking
through and around a corner "colored"

world war wall, looking
directly at me, un-momentarily.
Excuse me mister, but ...?

My silence deeper than
the Southern plantation house yard
Negro
Black Sambo
patience of
me not knowing what
in a-grocery-store-aisle to say,
the time of day.

What year is this year, anyway?
2018 is not that far away from 1863
in retrospect and reality. Me,

my silence longer than ... .

Excuse me sir, but ... ?

And I thought about how dirty white
his little used-to-be Clorox white

white socks were, dancing,
almost dangling
off his little white feet.
And I thought about

how dirty blond
his dirty blond hair was.

Taken by no surprise, a photograph:
The velvet blue beauty of
redneck poverty
looking straight at me
dressed to grocery shop

in my English tweed,
English
professor jacket,
un-matching vest,
faded blue
as my blue jeans.

A little boy's life looking
at me though the kind eyes of
sentimentality,
the science of ... love.

And I thought about
how small the world must be to see me
from the backseat of
a standard sized grocery cart
in a Bi-Lo grocery store
on a normal, ordinary,
cloudy Tuesday afternoon in late June.

Four years old,
maybe he was five,

beautiful,
a little kind face,
sunshine eyed white boy

facing forward
in a backwards
sounding, backwards leaning white
is "right" white world

that circles precisely the same sun
as anyone
in this grocery store
on that, a partly cloudy Tuesday
afternoon.

A kind face,
a kindergarten student
in a kindergarten grocery store
cart seat asking
a simple kindergarten question.

Excuse me sir, but ...?

A little beautiful whiter-than-white
white boy,
curious as a car mechanic
trying with all his heart
to diagnose
what he sees, vividly,
from a poor, white, trailer park perspective
as a problem,

a color-line arithmetic problem
wider than

his double-wide trailer park world of
ugly love and toy Tanka trucks,
Matchbox mixed completely up
Nascar racing cars and
Chattanooga shoeshine boy, Choo-Choo,
Christmas tree trains
circling
race-racing,
around racist railroad tracks.

In the background and the foreground,
railroad crossing signs
and white crosses burning,
blinking stop-light red.

"Excuse me Mister ..."

For what seemed like five minutes,
I thought and I thought and I thought
about
why
at his age, he already
knows
the score,
knows
how to count
hard
Christmas

candy
on his fingers.

He already knows
there is no Santa Claus
coming down
the chimney of
his ugly love,
a trailer park house.

He knows his primary colors do not
include my color,

knows he does like grits or rice or collard greens,
knows that niggers are only, yes only, supposed to be,
especially,
Saturday morning
cartoon
characters on TV and are not

supposed to be real people
who are
really real nice
and dressed real nice
like college professors and poets
in the grocery store wide aisles of America.

That little boy knows
it all because
his good looking, big, white,
beautiful white

mama
done told him so. Then and now
his good looking, big, white,
beautiful white
mama

is just far enough away, down, then up
the grocery store aisle not
to hear,
un-gracefully, her own delusional white
is "right"
white beautiful voice
telling him not to talk to,
especially,
colored people strangers
in grocery store
can vegetable aisles.

His mama,
beautiful, big, but not so fat as
a reasonable question mark
marking
her own favorite spot
in her,
on her
poor white trashcan world of
having just enough
grocery shopping money and Visa card,
nigger people food stamps
to stamp out

her own white trash poverty
today, one day at a time.

Beautiful face,
that little boy's mama
standing like a standing ovation
at a country music, Dwight Yoakam concert,
pound for pound,
crossways, standing,
reading calendars of calories,
counting, then recounting
the sum of
square carrot roots,
counting
the diet-tree dares of food labels
on the backside of
ugly love,
a can of Delmonte cream style corn.

From the way she shops, patiently,
counting vegetable aisle cans, I can tell
without
any redneck hint of any doubt
that she's had three weddings
without
a diamond clustered carat ring
in the last 5 years or so
and I know by the love for her baby boy
shining
lonesome in her pool water blue eyes,
she's still looking

for some kind of diamond ring, even if it's fake,
a mistake,
to sing
a love song to nobody else but
her 'cause she really is beautiful
from my slanted
grocery store slanted
Negro angle.

Another photograph, the same and different: The velvet
blue beauty of
redneck poverty looking at me
through the eyes of
sentimentality, the pure natural science of...
ugly love.

Her now, unhandsome, broad shouldered husband,
will do for now if not
forever
will she love and cherish and be faithful to thee.

He, her unhandsome husband, overly proud as
no purpose at all
votes conservative because he has nothing left
to conserve,
votes republican because he and his neckline red
redneck
is not navy blue,
but
his Ford F150 pickup truck is colored hate heavy
nigger dark blue

and you know tonight he is somewhere
this get-fucked-up evening
like any other get-fucked-up evening
fucked up drunk,
as they say, a skunk
still
constructing paradigm
homes and nice houses for rich, white mortgage
buyers.

Hammers, crowbars, screws and nails live,
meant to be,
quite content, quite trailer-park
content
in the pockets of his work day dirty pants.

Screw drivers and needle nose pliers live,
meant to be,
quite trailer-park content
in the rolled up portion of
his short sleeved Crimson Tide colored Alabama
tight T-shirt
tight as
white
is "right" tight
as the wrong season for wearing the looseness of
a bad-boy, Harley boy fit.

Defiance, he wears his life not
to fit.
He is a "rebel" with a beyond James Dean cause.

He whistles "Dixie"
in his sleep to keep from sleeping sound
in his double wide trailer
court sized,
queen sized,
dirty white sheet, white
bad, white
boy bed beside his beautifully fat white wife.

"Excuse me Mister, but is you..."
"Excuse me, sir..."

And I thought about the dirty dirt road
trailer-park trailer
that little white boy calls home.

And I thought about
his snotty nose, white half-brother and sister,
six and seven, just as dirty blond, lined up
white
as Holiday Bowling Center bowling pens
in the dirty
white
comfort of a double-wide sofa couch
watching
without
a hint of impending storm warning,
watching
flat screen television people flatten out reality,

flat as pancake luck
poured over
pancake love
flowing like pure Auntie Mama (nigger) maple
slow syrup

up not down into the crossed-up blue eyes
of a crossed-up
white trailer-park God

they can't wait to see every Sunday morning
their crossed-up
white
trailer-park God sends into their crossed-up white
trailer-park
country cream corn country life style. All the while
watching
a 42 inch wide commercial appeal,

a steal, rent to own,
$17.00 a week for two years and
one half
off the last full payment if paid in full on time,
the sacred duration of...forever.

A steal, commercial appeal selling
As Seen on TV
Honey Boo-Boo fashioned
white
trashcan
white

lying trashcan lids
designed exclusively to cover up the smell of
white
trash trailer park
trashcans.

They and them are ordinary, an ordinary
white family of
just ordinary kids, three dogs and a cat
named Cat
just sitting,
just waiting for the sun
to completely sit
down kindly for dinner, supper
at a trailer-park dining room table
much too small to smile. Still
they laugh because
they have nothing
better to do but wonder
what color makes the world go 'round
the sun one year at a time.

Daylight Savings Time saves no time
this time any time soon.
The moon is for dogs to bark at.
This they know
for the Bible told them so.

"Excuse me mister..."

And what seemed like five more
minutes, I thought about Tupelo, Mississippi.

Elvis Aaron Presley singing smooth
as his velvet Negro voice,
coming in loud, clear
on that little boy's trailer-park
stereo, a beaten down radio,

Love Me Tender,
Goodtime Charlie's Got the Blues

back-dropped, un-neatly, in prime time
6 o'clock television news:
Another random nigger in handcuffs,
dread locks locked up
too tight to be innocent of
the randomly routine charge of

shooting another random nigger
in his front-page-newspaper black face.

And I thought about Jesus of Nazareth
walking next to Elvis Aaron Presley
in Memphis, walking 'cross the muddy top of
the Mississippi River

and I thought about Johnny Lee Hooker,
all hooked up
to an electric boogie man,
letting that guitar

do all the talkin',
walkin' up and down
Mississippi railroad tracks, stepping
to the rhythms of
delta black blues,
overalls rolled up, wearing no shoes,
playing some of that muddy water
Mississippi
mud-water blues, no new Negro news.

Johnny Lee and Elvis Presley
trying,
crying,
dying
to tell me something I am trying to understand
about the nuanced beauty of
American poverty
that looks a lot like me.

"Excuse me sir, but is you ah ...?"

And I thought about
the packs and packages of plastic,

Ball Park hotdogs, America's pastime,
and Ball Park
hotdog buns in that little kid's cart.

And I thought about macaroni
with real cheese, potato chips, green
onion dips

and Pepsi Cola and Coca Cola and Diet Dr.
Pepper and the three cases of cold, very cold
Miller High Life,
American brewed, cheap, beer.

They and you are not supposed to use
Food Stamp
cards to pay for and/or how

three cases of High Life slipped under
the radar. I thought about

a frozen pizza, Tombstone Original,
(Do not thaw before baking at 425 for 18-20 minutes).

Don't forget, now you hear,
to set the stove-top timer. "Johnny B. Good"
Chuck Berry said
in a song to his guitar
with a dead pan Chuck Berry grin.

And I thought about
their ugly, used car out there
crying,
trying,
dying to be pretty used up
in the dead hot heat of
a hot Bi-Lo parking lot.

All four tires under inflated, dehydrated,
hoping
a carwash lives somewhere nearby.

A beaten up, beat-up blue, but sad
smiling blue Buick Regal
three times the age of that little boy
playing now,
pretending to be Superman,
Batman,

a John Wayne movie boy scout, saluting
now, inquiring "...is you..."

now from the backseat of
a Bi-Lo grocery shopping cart,
eating an unpaid for Pop Tart.

And I thought about
that little boy's bad pit bull laughing-face
dogs.
All three of them tied by nope-nigger rope
every day
out in that little boy's pit bull trailer park,
no grass, front yard.
All three of them,
just pit bulls barking at no moon
in their daylight sky.

Why is always a question?
Pitied out, pitiful pit bulls

just barking,
just waiting
for that little boy to come home,
smiling
a cavity candy eating, grocery store smile,
grinning
from ear to ear to eye because
he is happy, because
he is loved so much by his big,
fat, beautiful mother. Photograph:

The velvet blue beauty of redneck poverty,
sentimentality, the science of...love.

And I thought about
my own mother, she never told me
she loved me and I never told her either.
I have never been brave enough
to ask why because, I guess, we all bend
the ideas of what is true.

Do we really want to know
what we don't talk about when we don't
talk about love?

And for what seemed like five more minutes,
I thought about myself
as a kid in the back and front yards of my young life,
sweeping stubborn dirt
under a rug of
thinly sliced love,

growing up under oak branches
that loved me
like I was a baby tree just waiting to be. You see
my own beautiful mother never told me
she loved me
and I never could remember
my own beautiful mother's favorite
love song. Who was wrong?

And I thought about that little white boy,
honest
as any angel. That little white boy smiling
bright as star light on a moonless,
dark nigger dark night,
shining bright
from his little backwards world,

a backwards back seat of ugly love,
a Bi-Lo grocery shopping cart,
eating an unpaid for Pop Tart.

That little white boy, a photograph,
the sacred beautiful art of redneck poverty.

That little white boy, a little master
in Southern mannerism and Southern hospitality.

"Excuse me mister...," he said.

So when I almost immediately answered
that little white boy, I had been looking through

a little "White" Webster dictionary
for years "now,"
looking for a definition that definitively defines.

Thinking,
rethinking,
thinking at that moment
for what seemed like I don't know

how many minutes or how many times I have
tried relentlessly
to remember where,
what and who
white America categorized
the likes of me to be,
the likes of me to see,
the likes of me to say
in the aisles of a Bi-Lo grocery store.

"Excuse me mister, but is you a nigger?"
"Yes sir, yes sir, today in America, yes sir,
my little, white, beautiful blue eyed, buddy boy,
yes sir, I do believe I am."

BEFORE AND AFTER THE AFTERMATH: 9X11 = 23

The United States themselves are essentially the greatest poem.

— Walt Whitman

Everything begins at the beginning. Therefore, the tragedy of Gotham looks

all the way back to Y1K +92y = $\frac{1776}{13}$ stars divided by 13 faded stripes

draped over dead noise $\frac{\text{now}}{\text{yesterday}}$ divided by $\frac{\text{tomorrow}}{\text{if}}$ it comes

again into that blue Gotham City morning of remembering how civil a civil

war refuses to be. Y1K+800+65y divided by 2= 1 nation
under God

speed = $\frac{\text{distance}}{\text{time}}$ divided by $\frac{\text{time}}{\text{speed}}$ = . Times Square clock stopped,

but, still, light travels in a straight line.

Tyrone was still asleep on a Central Park bench.

Nancy was standing in front of the front office coffee pot.

Tom was driving into the City, late for work.

Timothy was putting on her makeup without a mirror.

An Al-Qaeda trigonometry of right triangles turned abruptly left and left all

seats empty. -2 World Trade Center Towers + a field adjacent Stonycreek

township, Pennsylvania, zip code, 1592something + the Pentagon = 4 airline

flight plans changed in mid-flight.

So $\frac{\text{N}}{\text{O}}$ = no x $\frac{\text{zero}}{\text{zero}}$ at ground level zero = $\frac{\text{Man}}{\text{Hat}}$ = Tan black billowing

black smoke billowing into the choking history of… Y1K 941 $\frac{\text{FD}}{\text{R}}$ still

with us, still smoking a pipe. $\frac{\text{December}}{\text{Pearl Harbor}}$ Nothing to fear but fear itself.

Raj had just missed his train.

Cora Castro was stuck in LA traffic, Allyson

was breast feeding her new baby. The captain has turned off the seat belt sign.

4 billowing black smokes attributable to the angry distorted distribution

of $\frac{\text{Osama Bin}}{\text{Laden}}$ x 4 FLTs of compressed refried confusion

divided by Jesus inverted without warning to Allah x 9x11= 23.

Allah Jesus

When velocity is constant, displacement varies directly with the names of

2 First Ladies, an almost First Lady and the Queen of Martin Luther,

Mary Lincoln—Jacqueline Kennedy—Ethel Kennedy--Coretta Scott King

2 First ladies, an almost First Lady and the Queen of Martin Luther

crying the same 4 tears over again. Meanwhile

Taniesha was dropping off the kids at day care.

Tyrone, asleep on a bench.

The captain has turned off the...

Ali Baba was waiting for the bank to open.

Oliver had just missed his train, he misses his two daughters. He misses

sleeping in his bed. He misses his life. He does not miss his wife.

Mary Ann was still counting sheep,

Simultaneous quadratic explosion on National TV, I was drinking a second

cup of coffee, a break between teaching university classes.

Lady Liberty, herself

resigned into the statue of..<u>What</u>
If

it were just another normal New York City morning leaf falling from a Big

New Amsterdam Apple tree.

Willie Lee was standing on the corner of theater-Playbill Street,

47nd and Broadway drinking a beer

from a brown paper bag when he heard

the smoke singing a sad song. He thought it was B B King singing

the blues   up and across   125th Street

next door to the Apollo.   He didn't know the show

was dead-still.

Shenika was shoplifting pampers and formula,   her baby girl turned

7 weeks old yesterday

in Gotham City Proper.   Nobody in the city will give her a job.

The Phantom of the Opera was taking an off Broadway, backstage

smoke break.

Billy Mae was taking   a taxi down to Tribeca

for a breakfast meeting   with a gay-day-date.

Miss Cora Mae's boy was stealing again,   in the back, side room

taking money out of

Mr. Mc Donald's cash register.   Tyrone was still asleep on a bench.

Francis Scott Key was singing off key.

The Star Spangled Banner, reduced   to a voiced-over red,

white and blue   clean up the blood Rag-Time-Song.

AK47 + 1= AK48 + 2 = 50 United States of confusion lowered

at half-mast

or mass greater than and/or equal to

the sum of static in the pockets of   19 boys.

5+ 14 or 9+10 or 7+11 or 17 + 2 or 16 + 3 or 18 + 1 =

all 19 box-cut boxes cut not to fit

underneath the seat or in the overhead compartment.

19 dead Muslim boys,

19 DOA cigarette boys.

19 dead boys + 4 dead airline flights

diverted = 9 x 11= 23.

NBC CBS ABC FOX BBC 93. 5 FM divided by C = CNN
N square

September 11, 2001,

an American working class Tuesday morning,

uninvited thunder

multiplied -1,492 divided into 1,776 stars, then

add 2,001 stripes =1you and 1me
9x11 = 23

Live from Ground Zero, New York City, "This is Bryant Gumbel,

I'm down on 59th and 5th, where are you?"

Miss Jones was taking morning attendance.

Oliver Joe was drunk, waiting for the liquor store to open.

Ed, walking home after night shift when he saw the smoke.

Billy Ray was tending his livestock in   Daybreak, Nebraska

Ava Batts was still fast asleep, still dreaming.

The captain has turned off the...

Every report, the exact same, 3,000 dead.

Light travels in a straight line.   4

lines of morning angry air,

no easy despair spilled onto FAA flight plan of...

30,000 feet and still climbing.

You are now free to move about the cabin. In case of

an emergency, your seat cushion can be used as a flotation device.

OBAMA'S CHILDREN

(As told by one who rides Nikki Giovanni's Night Wind)

Dear Stationary White Stationery,
I write to you from the point of view of a light-weight
paper weight. I am standing right out here waiting
for you to   EXIT
our local *Zip Store*-gas station so, conveniently, I can
inquire upon you, Sir.

"Excuse me Sir, but Sir, can you spare any spare
change" to spare my Negro-ology-disparity this afternoon?

I use big words, Sir, because I have a small vocabulary.
Inherited habit causes me to refer to you as such, Sir. I
take that you understand, Sir, 'cause

uncelebrated skin-color-coated habit is a hard habit
to break evenly
into the "bad uneven words" I have no choice but
to repeat out here on a begging-daily basis, yes Sir.

In too many *Made In America* ways, people like me
are still, in your mind and in the minds of too many,
cotton patch people, waiting on wagon wheels to roll
us towards indigo farms and tobacco fields aplenty,
sorta like slavery days.
You don't believe me because you believe me, so I'll
say it again like a blues John Lee Hooker love song.
You don't believe me
because

you believe me. Yes sir, you believe me and in me
because
I am the color of wet sandpaper-sunburnt black,
because
I wear my ball cap backwards so you can't tell
whether I am coming in or going out. You believe me, Sir,
because
I drink only tall cans of Miller Lite, Bud Light, Coors
Light, Natural Light and Old Milwaukee
beer from a Negro brown
boy paper sack every day the Good Lord sends my way.

Jesus and His Mother, Miss Mary probably won't mind
being my witnesses
when I say to you, Sir, what it is I say: Like Blue magic
parades of marching children,
out of nowhere, out of everywhere they came announcing
the beautiful unannounced-ments of themselves,
Obama's Children.

They look just like regular boys, regular girls next door.
Whether you live in the "Hood" as I do or
on top of a red Mercedes Benz hood as you do,
right next door
to you, to me they live. Ordinary, but they are not.

This they, I speak now of, were gifted by a gracefully
laced royal grace, then wrapped like Christmas, carefully,
in the colors of   compassion colored paper.
I know you don't believe me, now, do you Sir? Listen, Sir,

I know I ain't never been to nobody's college. And to you, I know without any doubt, I look like I just dropped down from outer space, a real nigger Neil Armstrong that looks more like Louis Armstrong blowing into a jazzy trumpet Beale Street breeze. Please listen to me, Sir. I know I look like I never read a book, but

I have a GED Ph. D in the science of Niggernometry-
Biology. I dissect bullshit instead of bull frogs, thus
the high educated cutting guess of gambling words, I use.
The cacophony of hyperbole, I
use big words because I have a small vocabulary
and besides that's just me and my straight-no- chaser
way of just looking at just what I see,
what you refuse to see,
a rosebud bursting into bloom in the spring of rainy years,
Obama's children.

The springtime of America's her-stories reads, reveals
Hip-Hop kids,
beat-box kids,
backpack kids,
skateboard kids,
computer whiz kids,
Superchildren,
Obama's children.

They are Obama's legacy. You see, they turned 10, 11,
13 and 14
between 2 Novembers exactly 8 years apart. They were
born again in those years "between"

the breezes of
a Maya Angelou song and a Maya Angelou poem.
From the mouth of his wind
of words,
they heard velour coated verbs, nickel plated platinum
nouns, sterling silver conjunctions connecting
the adjectives of liquid pure gold that flowed, then paused
stately and heavenly as Venus, herself, disguised as a star.

They heard President Barack Obama's velvet voice calling
forth the favor and flavor of just "Be yourself and practice
within and outside of, love."

This *Blue Hope Diamond* shaped love, I hear every day
in the way Obama's children smile. I know you don't
believe me, now do you Sir? Look, I don't blame you.
Blame yourself, Sir, if you need to frame blame. Be sure
to hang it on your nice, corner office
wall so everybody can see it   except you, Sir.

Look at me, wearing brand new high top converse
tennis shoes and a torn up life. You don't believe.
I don't believe myself 3 quarters of the time, but
3 Thomas Jefferson quarters and 4 Franklin D.
Roosevelt dimes is all I need
to talk you into buying me a cold, cheap can of cheap
Old Milwaukee beer.

Make no mistake, I know I'm not a reliable narrator.
How do I know what I am speaking of. I heard them
college boys talking about reliable narrators

in the assigned short stories they try not to read, so
I know I am not one, I know I am not reliable.
I also know a calculator has no default.
I know, Sir, how you multiply
my blood shot eyes only to the 1st power. And why is it

that your subtraction of my jazz song is always wrong?
Long division problems in America are too long to divide
when you, Sir,
hide the sums of addition so I can't see the theory
of the string so many of us dark people dangle from
like puppets.   Negro life with a pocket knife
is a Jesse B. Simple life when viewed upside down.
In this city, we live
by the hour. Minutes don't matter
to the shatter and scatter of ricocheted AK bullets.
You don't believe me because you believe in me
and what you perceive as my left-over-from-slavery
red raggedy red ways of pulling empty red wagons
across white fields of cotton aplenty. Any way out is,
precisely, how I got in, how I get in-to your head, Sir.

So listen up, pull up a Lazy Boy, white lifestyle, white
reclining, white leather chair
and listen to the way
a Negro heart beats when it is not beating.

No, I'm not a poet, not a prophet, I am a promise.

Since the chicken factory shut down, I now work
odd, uneven jobs.

Most weeks I am unemployable 6 days out of 7.
No, truth is I ain't looking for no work no more.
I have been rejected seventeen times too many times,
divided by and into
the way I talk and walk these begging streets. And
that equals exactly what you, Sir, want it to equal.

My knees are sore, I pray, but I ain't been to see
Mr. Jesus in a long time.   Sunday morning
is just the seventh day of a get-drunk week for me.

I know I look like I am, but I am not homeless.
It's just that where I stay is not a nice home
with nice floral print kitchen curtains letting in
sunlight and reminding me to close them at night.

My life is an open curtain life, open all the time so
the Night Winds can blow in easy as winter weather
looking for cracks
in my curtains of conversation with you, my dear
sad Sir. You
have it made because everything was/is already
Made In America for you, Sir.   Now, take me,

I live two blocks up the street from the University
of Tennessee at Chattanooga. I live damn near next door
to a zoo, an *Animal House* movie,
a frat boy house,
built beautifully amongst "race" ruins of my street.

Fraternity boys, they like me. I love talking to them.
We drink the same kind of cheap beer every night
of the week 'cause weekend nights are just that, another
drinking-stay-up-all-night-frat-boy night. I hear them
through the wall cracks of my boarding house room.

We live (I stay) next to the same railroad track sign.
We listen to the same loud-ass train track noise.
We watch the same parade of made-up Barbie Doll,
partying white girls praying parents don't find out
the real price for missing too many 8 o'clock classes.

We step over the same sidewalk cracks, and when
we are drunk, we stumble
into the same border grass, but they smoke more pot
than I can afford
with the small change I get from you, Sir . "Excuse me..."

I see just about every student in every class
just about every day. Pennies from their tuition fee,
they hand-out to me. They are, without knowing, paying
me for the other side of their reality show "real"
public college education.
No text books required. Sun Drop-Welfare Science
is a take-home final exam that cannot be graded
by a rubric cube science. Too many holes in the formula,
too many mixed-up colors to align on a one-sided square.

No, I am not a poet, I am a preposition playing out of
position. I don't know my place, never did. I am drunk
as a drunk shrunk on a Wednesday afternoon,

the 15th day of May. I
am just looking, not reading, just looking
like just looking at a book,
seeing those you've forgotten how to see, Sir,
the sunshine faces of super sunlight children,
Obama's children.

I have no hope. They need no hope because
they are hope, our hope. Baptized at birth
in African American Holy River water, they know
not of
night nigger people assigned
as such and such and such as you do, Sir.

They are not afraid of love. They are *Bold as Love*
like Jimi Hendrix playing an upside down guitar
with his teeth, then pouring kerosene on the flame.
Obama's children have built a new fire in America.

They, quietly, leave blank, on purpose, the race-
space on college and other application forms.
They laugh at you, Sir, redrawing race-war lines,
re-stereotyping a stereo-typical-mind-set,
building a Mexico wall, going backwards in time
but not in space. To them, you are, Sir,

a Mr. Day-Light-Saving-Time man, trying to save
a time in American history
that cannot
be saved
in the name of a Religious Right which is,

was wrong
long before race-wall-baseball was invented in 1776.

But do not let the syncopated cadence of my jazz
fool you, Sir. Just you listen a bit more now, you hear.

No, as I have already made un-abundantly unclear,
I am not a poet,
I am poor as a locked door when you can't get in
or out even with a perfectly cut key. Me,
I know you don't trust anything
I say because you don't know how to trust
what I say when I say.... Obama's children,

They know without further final examination
or explanation in modern day political terms.
They know that the 2nd Amendment is not an AK-47
box of hollow point bullets
and empty shell casings
scattered, blindly, across a school room floor.

Obama's children,
they, too, walked the crowded classroom hallways
out of
and into the front door of
Columbine, Colorado, the front door of
Sandy Hook Elementary School, the front door of
Stoneman Douglas High School. They know, exactly,
what you refuse to know, Sir.

Obama's children, they know
that what you say on a television set, Sir, is not, not,
not, not what Thomas Jefferson meant,
not what Alexander Hamilton meant,
not what James Madison meant,
not what John Hancock's signature signed
up to mean. And they know that you know

that's not what the Founding Fathers
meant when you proclaim what you, so loudly,
proclaim in the name of God. Which God (?)
is a hard question for you to answer isn't it, Sir?

Obama's children,
they are, at this trying, surreal moment
in the United States of American history, a legacy,
years beyond the time they should've been sent.
They know
not without laughter
can race-bigotry be depicted as me and just me
and a bunch of Mexicans America does not want
to keep. According to you, Sir, America only needs
enough Mexicans to pick fruit and mow lawns.

It's a strange kind of strange fruit hanging
from a strange fruit tree. Most of Obama's children
have never
heard the voice of Billie Holiday sing, but they know
the lyric by heart.
They know the un-art of slavery. They know
the four corners of Confederacy is not art at all

as it is purported to be. Me and just me and Mexico
doing our Saturday night ghetto-el barrio no-step
forward dance is all you allow yourself to see, Sir, but

Obama's children,
they know African American History Month
is every moment, every hour, every day,
every week,
every fortnight,
every month of an American calendar year.

Obama's children,
they are not afraid of love.
They are not afraid to acknowledge and celebrate
all that was given to America by the Negro. They
know the real history of Texas and New Mexico.
They know the size of a Native American/Indian
Reservation
Casino
is measured by the weight of Andrew Jackson $20
bills. They know.

Obama's children,
they are Harry Potter people.
They grew up watching and seeing the world
through round, black-brown rimmed eye glasses.

Obama's children,
they know the star-shine-light they see at night
is coated by human acid made mistake.
They take no grains of salt for granted. They know.

They grew up riding Day Rave skateboards
at all times of day and night
in forbidden parking lot light.

With no caution to the fall, they all
are the definitions of the surf-board-balance of
wave-walking on blue water.
They cry when it hurts,
they laugh when it's funny.
They still watch cartoons, *Looney Tunes,*
Rugrats, Scooby Doo, Sponge Bob Square Pants.

A rainbow does not know it's a rainbow, but
Obama's children, they know.
Kind laughter, their eyes tell me so, so I know.

But what do I know when all you see, Sir, when
you look at me is me, just me,
an ordinary nigger grown-man-boy standing
outside of a gas station waiting
on an earthquake to make my poverty shake,

rattle and roll up the sleeves of a short sleeve shirt
that once had long sleeves. Re-Skirting the truth
is re-hand-me-down political science book ideology.

Them college boys call me Professor Sandwich 'cause
I love ham and cheese, but Sand Trap's my nickname.
According to Invisible Man in the novel *Invisible Man,*
nicknaming is the deadly art black of escape. This town
only allows me to escape

not from but into another reason to escape,
if you know what I mean, Sir. You think I look like I
don't know how to read, never read a book, but let me
tell you something, Sir. Jail time is book reading time.

Some call me Junior boy, but most people call me Sand
Trap 'cause I bogie 18 holes, routine as routine is regular.
My putting 7 iron was born curved the wrong way and
I'm left handed and dyslexic. Big advantage when
most days around here are upside down and backwards.

Still I ain't never been able to land a golf ball anywhere
near landing a golf ball on the greens. The fairway
ain't never been fair to me. You know, as they say,
too dark to pay to park in the Mountain City Country
Club Membership parking lot. But,
but nothing. I am
man in a cage, a baseball (spring training) batting cage,
trying to hit each day
as hard as I can, hoping
for a hole in one
of my socks not to be noticed
by the *Hamilton Co. Coroner's Report* of
a dead nigger
found dead, leaning up against a street light, dead-light
post. Backdrop noise, ugly dead remixed music
rolling towards the end of my credits.

But Obama's children refuse to hear the dead-
talking weight of unfaithful remixed lyrics, refuse
to learn to read the proud, white

sheet music of raining
racism and left-over other 1950s isms like sex

and the extra ugly weight of baggage, unclaimed,
going and going
around, around and around and, around
conveyor belts called   Baggage Claim
on the ground floor of every airport in America.

Obama's children
carry onto airplane flights the carry-on science of
packing a backpack like packing a small suit case.
They count their airline ticket blessings without
counting them. No calculator needed.
They fly first class in coach class
because they don't believe in first in class (caste
system science of living in America).

They know Rosa Parks, her first and her last name.
They silently earplug-out noise pollution,
the wailing tunes of 3K air traffic control
discrimination,
anticipation of no landing gear. *no fear* is a T-shirt.
They don't believe in the   "White Myth."
They believe in   Blue Magic.
In ways I can't quite articulate, they seem to believe
as the children of the 60s   believed
in the science of
peace, love, flowers, forgiveness. Obama's children,

they wear overnight panda bear pajama pants
in and on day-light flight patterns. They retro-love
the Rolling Stones, the Beatles, the Who. They
dance to Motown as we did and do. They know
Marvin Gaye and Diana Ross. They know metal
detectors cannot detect
the "rock" or the "roll" or the "soul" of music.

They wear torn-up, winter plaid flannel
shirts in 4th of July, August heat
not because they're cold but
because they're cool as Colored people cool.

They are not afraid of love. They wear worn-out
Tuesday boots that should have been tossed out
Monday morning, not-too-soon, not because they
can't afford new ones but because
they have learned to afford to listen to lyrics:

Imagine there's no country, it isn't
hard to do, nothing to kill or die for.

Just as the Book of John Winston Lennon sang,
Obama's Children sing with the Queen of Soul,
Aretha Franklin's gospel lyrics:

Gotta find me an angel to fly away with me.

They sing along. An easy, every school day
morning technology children's choir, they are.

They *Lift Every Voice and Sing* like James Weldon
Johnson, sweet-ly, that old Negro gospel spiritual.

In the quiet force of their voices, if we listen, they
teach the teaching of pure ecological examination.

Obama's children, they save the planet by being
the planet. They know, I know, and you know,
Sir, that naturally green grown organic produce
should not be naturally green
grown organically overpriced to the point of....

They vote mostly blue because they want to breathe
clean air, drink fresh tap water the way we all used to.

But who are they, these beautiful strangers, angels
flying without the notice of wings,   celebrating
the diversity of being diverse,
and why am I standing out here, begging for dimes,
wearing high top black converse shoes,
conversing
with a white sheet of white paper, stationery
as ordinary concrete?   Ordinary

just like me, an ordinary out-figured-out "figger"
on an ordinary afternoon,
standing off to the front left-hand side of ordinary,
looking into the eyes of an ordinarily crowded
zip-right-up,
zip-right-in,
zip-right-out, Middle Eastern Muslim owned

convenient store-gas station, asking ordinary,
everyday, zipped-up mouth customers if they
have any ordinary,
leftover,
loose pocket change to spare.

"Excuse me Sir, excuse me Ma'am,"
I say in my killingly beautiful, scary, Negro, deep,
muddy Mississippi River, slave holding state, accented
Southern
charming voice,
"Excuse me, excuse me Sir, excuse me Ma'am, but
do you...would you like to...? Can you
help a brother out this afternoon? Sure is a nice day,
glad it stopped raining.
Thank you Sir, thank you Ma'am, have a blessed day,
God bless you
and you too. Take care now, you hear."

Shark shaking, Southern natured fear of me:
A white business man
dressed up in a white business man suit,
handing to me a folded green dollar bill, smiling
a big grin because he's afraid not to smile.

Under my breath, yes, I laugh, I laugh at his cheap,
brown, wingtip, tipping J C Pen-nae shoes, tied up
too tight   to breathe. Patterned leather
for the impending weather, his shoes, a perfect fit.

He's sheet-white clueless. I laugh, but...because
every Black man in America knows that wearing
cheap dressed-for-church shoes
steals all of the expense of
wearing an expensive suit. It's all about the jazz.

You've never liked me, Sir, but you love me
and my musical ways. I know you listen to Coltrane
and Bessie when no one is looking. I know you love
the easy Sunday morning
way I play big band piano notes between brown
pennies, quarters and the thin weight of a dime.

Crime is my first, second and third cousin   removed
(the next of kin) 'cause crime rhymes with time served.
No, I am not a poet,   I am ex-poisonous.
4 years, 2 months, 16 days
in Angola for riding a borrowed bicycle for exercise
on the wrong side of the road is my prison number.

I would love to vote, but a *Felony* on my parole sheet
tells me I no longer possess the mindset to place a bet
on who the next president should be.   So, Sir,

on the second Tuesday in November each election year,
look and you will see me
or someone who looks like me just standing out here
in front of this store, flashing
a stereotypical Negro grin exclaiming, "Excuse me
Sir, but...excuse me Ma'am, but... sure is a nice day."

My tobacco stained yellow teeth ain't never been
gleaming, Colgate toothpaste white. They have always
been more like Washington D C Watergate white
at night breaking into dreams of breaking out of....

In my never-been-humble opinion, politics ain't nothing
but a white mailbox box full of   white people tricks.
Nigger boy life in a white mailbox
on the side of a rural American road is a love story if
you like love-horror stories told from the voice of
a cardboard box leaning up against
a cold city street on a cold winter night.

Kicked like a football all of my life, I've been.
I have never, not once, been allowed to drift
through the up-rights for extra points scored
on a Friday night,
Saturday afternoon
or on Sunday after church.   The song,

I've always known the National Anthem rigged me
to lose long before kickoff, still
I take my hat off,
place my hand over my heart
and listen to the beating lyrics
of Francis Scott Key every chance I do not get.

I know I look like I don't know the full moon from
a jar full of moonshine, but...
and yet, Obama's children,

they look at me, none of this they see. My face is lined out,
painted in hardness, but they are not afraid of my sadness.

Obama's children, they smell, still, the flowers of
Michelle Obama's White House Rose Garden
where planted compassion of every color grew beautifully
tangled vines, cherry trees, peach tree branches of hope
and acknowledgement.

Without noticing, Obama's boys and girls still notice
a time when time, itself,
acknowledged global warming,
acknowledged the melting of the Arctic caps.

Obama's children, they see you, Sir, smoking
the burned-up coal burning smell of not giving a 3
dime damn about emissions.
They see you not acknowledging Women's Rights,
not acknowledging that Black Lives Matter. And I

acknowledge, Mr. White Piece of White Paper Jr.,
that under your white breathing breath,
you are saying right now, "Why, he makes sense
on paper, but
why is he sitting in the cockpit wearing a sky cap,
don't ya think he's too   dark,
too dumb to fly an airplane?" Let me remind you,
Mr. Blank Piece of White Paper, Sir, that I turn
aircraft carriers around on dimes with the sound
of soul music.

Go home and listen to Sam Cooke cook up a mess
of collards greens, then you'll know what I mean.

It sure is funny how, to you, a small, ragged hole
in the torn plaid short sleeves of my life is a gaping hole
in your United Airline trans-continental sky of
remembering,
understanding,
acknowledging that people, dark as dark blue,
have always lived on American Airport runways. We

have always been your luggage, your excess baggage,
your Negro cargo,
ghetto, "hood,"
you know, American 6 o'clock
News reality show showing up (you)
disguised as catching an alligator
with a police-night-stick-bullet-scattering-nigger-night
special on primetime television.   Revise the re-vision.

Obama's children, they are doing just that, revising.
They remind us all how easily the white myth of forgetting
forgot how beautifully wonderful
the Obama's White House years were,
forgot how Barak blue-shape-shifted
red recessed economic sadness into reasons of hope,
forgot how the whole wide world lit up when Barak smiled.

I can see him now, smiling beautifully that beautiful
Presidential smile,
walking like a jazz record recording itself, walking

towards Marine Helicopter One,
later to be transported to Air Force One,
later to land, perfectly, between piano and a song.

Barak Obama walked like jazz, talked like jazz. He
showed to white America the Negro, Black
African American,
Colored people color of swinging jazz notes.

And to this Colored people color when heard across
this land, the people danced,
some without knowing the steps.
Obama's dance changed how America sees the Negro.

The 6 pm o'clock Nigger News Negro definition of
Black people
all of a sudden
was not the only definition of African Americans.

A Black is Beautiful, Obama's face faced, eye to eye,
the largest white, receptive crowd in American history.
And the dancing people proudly, boldly reveled
in the ambiance of
a Reverence Dr. Martin Luther King colored sky.

Then one day while the children were dancing
on their father's White House lawn, the sky suddenly
turned dark. November, 2016. Seemingly
the weather people forgot how to predict the death of
a nation. *Birth of a Nation,* un-silently, was born again.

Only In America, the only people who saw it coming
as Klan-Killing-Kindness-Backlash(s)
were African Americans.
African Americans were not surprised because we know
the size and shape of a lynching tree is white-man-made,
not white-woman-made.

2016, November said to a cold December day, "We
need to rebuild the lynching tree, it can't be Hillary."

No, I am not a poet, not a prophet, but a promise.
I am what I am,
a Negro with thick lips and a wide open nose. I know,
exactly, the combed-over smell of racism.
Hurried yellow wooden hair burning smells,
exactly, as it has always smelled.
You don't believe me because you believe me, Sir.

The white myth of forgetting forgot, on purpose,
to remember the pure purple-ness of poetry.
Maya Angelou, wrapped in the new born smell of
Obama's baby blanket and Obama's baby shoes, told
the nation, The United States of America,
"When hope is dead, *Still I Rise.*"
African Americans were not surprised that November,
Wednesday (the day after) morning.

Every African Americans knows
why my shoes are untied on purpose,
know why my beard is untrimmed on purpose,

know why I wear my ball cap backward on purpose,
know, exactly, why

a lot of them rich white college boys love talking to me
as if 2 quarters and a dime held tightly together slide so
easily into the dark nigger nature of a vending machine.

As I told you, I see just about every student just about
every day, but almost never do I see a black professor
strolling proudly across campus carrying a satchel full of
college knowledge.

Maybe that's why some of them white college boys
call me *professor* as a joke they are not joking about.

Maybe they need me.
Maybe them rich white boys need me,
maybe, more than I need the thin weight of pocket change,
quarters, nickels, pennies and dimes. Maybe

I'll stop talking and tell you, exactly, what I was just about
to say about that day
the Reverence Dr. Martin Luther King Jr. clear blue sky
dropped,
the day the music stopped, and we stopped dancing, but
I won't. What I will tell you is this:

Obama's children kept dancing. They are still dancing
to an orchestra of love lyrics, unprintable
in black and white
pencil marks that mark a new day in America's history.

Sound waves travel forever and forever young
are the young ears pierced by Obama's words
of compassion and acceptance. They are not afraid of
love, and love is not afraid of them.

Take me for an example, Sir, if you need an example.
I dropped out of high school
before I dropped out of high school.
You know my story
well, Sir, better than most. But somehow I learned
to write insidiously sharp, cutting words,
pretty as a poet,
words that remind me that I talk too much.

So let me and it suffice to say, they, Obama's children
come quiet as an army of answers not questions.

They come wearing coats, jackets and hats of
pure understanding and forgiveness.
Their biological parents never once had to tell them
to honor our differences.
The President of the United States of America told them
and they listened.
They grew up riding skateboards, perfecting the ever elusive
science of balance, walking on water.
Race and gender equality is as natural for them
as a cool drink of spring bottled water
on a hot hiking-up-a-mountain day. They grew up royal
as Windsor Castle in a White House designed and decorated
by their African American,

Black,
Negro
Colored parents, Mr. and Mrs. Barack and Michelle Obama.
They grew up side by side with their sisters, Sasha and Malia.
They grew up listening to, learning from and   loving
Michelle's mother, their grandmother   Marian Robinson.

Their biological parents never had to tell them, "When
you grow up, you can be anything   you want to be."
The first Black President of the United States of America
showed them,
told them and they listened without ever knowing they
were   listening to what they were hearing:
The wonderful blooming and blossoming sounds flower
gardens make when flowers are watered long, deep, slow.

They learned early that the effects of an easy answer
is the easiest way to break a heart. They don't believe
as you believe, Sir.   Like so many, you
think that you can drink a bottle of poison and not die.
Why?
They don't ask us why, they tell us why, don't ask us how,
they show us how to love the blue color of blue magic.
They listen to the music of   love
in the voices of Lorde, 21 Pilots and Neon Trees. They

believe trees can be saved. They dismiss the stage play
of bigotry by not buying a ticket.
They know the melting pot
has been melting too long to not have melted yet.
They travel in groups diverse as the universe.

They count lucky stars without counting them.
They know without knowing that they know
Obama's last standing ovation is still standing.

The cadence of Obama's velvet voice still calls forth
his children. From every part of this country they ride
state boards,   balanced upon the center of
things   too many of us are afraid to acknowledge.

They know the chemical reaction to love is love. And

I love President Barack Obama. To me, he will always
be the quintessential   American Statesman.

I use big words because I have a small vocabulary. You
use big words to impress. But Sir, may I remind you,
that *Impressionism* paints and paintings are wordless.
Sincerely, yours truly,
Mr. Samuel S. Trap
PS,
Fyi
and just so you know: The American weather forecast,
from now on, will be predicted
by a diversity of pregnant weather women
giving birth to Obama's children's children. I know
you now know
you don't believe me, Sir, because you believe me, Sir.
Amen
I'll say it again like a blues John Lee Hooker love song.
Amen

DINNER WITH DOROTHY PARKER

Stars are soft as flowers and just as near,
she says,
here my dear lad, shall we sit, lazily, in late April,
this late afternoon
when moon and rainbow know
to occupy the same sky.
Why is it that it will not rain? she asks.

Thunder and rain is a refrain repeated now
for the polished
Manhattan people.
Time, sometimes, forgets the time of day, she says,

you know, somebody else played somebody
else's love song at this table,
in these very café chairs yesterday. I say little
between the soft cuts of her beautiful words.

Today I play Scott Joplin maple leaf rag
music, listening deep into the eyes of

New York City's society lady, Dorothy Parker,

as she is purported to be.

And me, I'm just a reflection, 1927.

I steal, openly, from the 5 'n' 10 cent store of

her soft-sex voice.

Dinner on the rocks, too early to get so drunk,

but, my dear lad, she says,

there are still kindly things

for me and for you to know.

There's so little in taking, so little in giving.

To have, there is little, but the things

you had in early days.

Once there was a rose, she says,

that faded young.

Yes indeed, years now since first

we saw the apple tree bear fruit.

How beautifully awful of us,

drinking coffee-cup-love from bourbon

glasses. How terribly kind

sad cafes sometimes are on rainy,
impending, summer weather afternoons
when rainy-day people see not a hint of love.

You love so much the sound of your own voice,
too much, also, do you
not, my dear lad? Tables can turn without
intending to turn.

Placed, our order of nothing but
more rocks.
Horribly Southern, sweet like tea,
our waitress with
her made-for-now made-up face.

Oh, let it be a night of lyric rain, she says,
softly, white as
a waitress still walking like she's still wearing
a red sleeping gown
carefully as a red ball room dance dress,
silk, cotton,

and nighttime lace,

a face long like a long time she's

been flying without landing,

circling concentric-ly sad wait table circles,

orbiting only the colors of commitment.

Love, she says, is sharper than stone

or stick.

Hold not upon the desire to be so sad, my dear

young lad. Lilacs

blossom also sweet as inscriptions

for painted ceilings of

bedrooms.

Love loves only the corners of any room.

Drink, dance, laugh and lie.

Die laughing if you can, my dear lad.

How dreadfully wonderful love can often be,

but never do we see

the color of *Arrangement in Black and White.*

Only, we see the crossed-out pages of the storyteller's
story book. Look
wise beyond what's beneath, beyond,
she says,
there was a rose that faded young,
they say of me,
and so as they should say of me. Dangerously
pretty that of the dark girl's rhyme,
the verse of writing defiant verse.
The evening primrose knows too much.
Chrysanthemums know nothing, she says.
Love is quick to come and quicker to go.
All my answers are inadequate. But you asked
about love, didn't you my dear?

If you must, then sit closer to me, she says.
Branch with me if you must climb
late April summer afternoons
over rocks and bourbon from the bottle.

So little, I offer
to you, my lad. Drink,
slowly, rocks of my rushing words.

With eager lip, I paint my mouth
a fragrant red, she says.
Attention to the question is dutifully
yours. Inadequately, my second
love was water
in a clear white cup.

First love always stops
suddenly
because there is always a rosemary
growing wild

and we all are due to fall in love again.
I remember, she says,
because behind my back they talk of me.

Such glorious filth
fills limpid eyes. Be it the friends

I may have slipped
and strayed, otherwise, why is it that when
I am in Rome.

Two be the things I am wiser to know:
(1) Helen of Troy
had a wandering glance.
(2) Here in my heart, I am Helen.

Joy stayed with me a fortnight. Hope,
it was that tutored
me. Perfectly ungrammatical,
love is a sung song. Eyes,

limpid, she says, are slant, slow,
do not know. Unseeingly,
the open eye. Always I have known,
no more my little song

comes back. All my answers are inadequate,
love is quick

and quicker to go. But you asked about love,
didn't you, love?
A dream lies dead here now. Softly,
my dear lad,
may you now go.
Stars are just as soft as flowers,
my dear, and just as near, she says

as her soft-sex voice fades into the impending
nature of afternoon rain pouring
pure blue jazz all over me.

ABOUT THE AUTHOR

EARL S. BRAGGS, UC Foundation and Herman H. Battle Professor of English at the University of Tennessee at Chattanooga, is the author of *Hat Dancer Blue,* winner of the 1992 Anhinga Poetry Prize selected by Marvin Bell. He is the author of these books from Anhinga Press: *Walking back from Woodstock, House on Fontanka, Crossing Tecumseh Street, In Which Language Do I Keep Silent, Younger than Neil, Cruising Weather Wind Blue and Syntactical Arrangement of a Twisted Wind.* He also is the author of *Boy Named Boy [a Memoir]* (Wet Cement Press) and *Obama's Children* (Madville Publishing).

"After Allyson," a chapter from his yet to be published novel, *Looking for Jack Kerouac,* won the 1995 Jack Kerouac Literary Prize. Other awards include Tennessee Arts Commission Individual Artist Grant and a Chattanooga Allied Arts Individual Artist Grant. Supported by Summer Fellowships from the University of Tennessee at Chattanooga, he has traveled and written in Russia, Ukraine, France and Spain. He is a native of Wilmington, North Carolina.